Just Ask a Woman

Just Ask a Woman

Cracking the Code of What
Women Want and How They Buy

Mary Lou Quinlan

WILEY

JOHN WILEY & SONS, INC.

Published by John Wiley & Sons, Inc., Hoboken, New Jersey.
Published simultaneously in Canada.

For general information on our other products and services please contact our Customer Care
Department within the U.S. at (800) 762-2974, outside the United States at (317) 572-3993
or fax (317) 572-4002.

Wiley also publishes its books in a variety of electronic formats. Some content that appears in
print may not be available in electronic books. For more information about Wiley products,
visit our web site at *www.Wiley.com*.

Library of Congress Cataloging-in-Publication Data
Quinlan, Mary Lou.
   Just ask a woman: cracking the code of what women want and how they buy / Mary Lou
   Quinlan.
      p.   cm.
   Includes bibliographical references and index.
   ISBN 0-471-36920-9 (cloth : alk. paper)
      1. Women consumers—United States.   2. Marketing—United States.
   3. Women—United States—Attitudes.   I. Title.
   HF5415.33.U6 Q56 2003
   658.8'34'082—dc21
                                                                        2002153132

Printed in the United States of America

10 9 8 7 6 5 4 3 2 1

To Mom
who taught me to listen with my heart

To Dad
who taught me to speak from my soul

CONTENTS

ACKNOWLEDGMENTS

As someone who loves to listen, I have been fortunate to listen to some extraordinary people throughout my career as well as during the research for and writing of this book.

My first thanks go to the people in my career who have had the greatest influence on my love for marketing and communications: Dr. Daniel N. DeLucca, my advertising professor and first boss at Saint Joseph's University; Diane Perlmutter, my Avon mentor and ongoing counselor; Jim Preston, retired chairman of Avon Products Inc.; Avon alumnae Phyllis Davis and Gail Blanke; ad agency leader Keith Reinhard of DDBNeedham New York Worldwide and the men who made Just Ask a Woman possible, my friends Roy Bostock and Craig Brown of the Publicis Groupe.

I want to thank the clients of Just Ask a Woman for giving me the opportunity to travel the country and listen to what women want, especially Steve Sadove and Christina Johnson of Saks Fifth Avenue, Lisa Caputo of Citigroup, Cheryl Callan of Ortho-McNeil Pharmaceuticals, Miriam Muley of General Motors, Carole Black of Lifetime Television, Anne Jackson and Andy Sareyan of AOL Time Warner, Cathie Black of Hearst Magazines, Beth Pritchard of Bath and Body Works, Dan Brestle and Pam Baxter of Estee Lauder, Gordon Bethune and Bonnie

Reitz of Continental Airlines, Suzanne DeWard of Kellogg's, Francesca Brockett of Toys R Us, Bill McComb of McNeil Consumer Products, and Jim Cascino of Discovery Toys. Their companies listen to women as a way of life, and their leadership makes their brands women-right as well as successful. Also I would like to send a sentimental thank you to the very first client of Just Ask a Woman, Gary Cormack of The Boots Company; a framed five pound note records our first earnings.

Writing a book about what women think is not a simple thing to do, especially for a first-time author. To the team at John Wiley & Sons, especially my editor Airie Stuart and her associate Jessie Noyes, I offer my thanks for their patience and talent and for their enthusiasm from the start. I also wish to thank Michelle Patterson, Emily Conway, Aditi Shah, and P. J. Campbell for getting the book from birth to bookstore and my agent Wes Neff, who called me after he read an article about me to say, "There must be a book in this." His conviction paid off. Finally, for putting me on the road, I appreciate Barbara Henricks and Mark Fortier of Goldberg McDuffie and Don Walker and the wonderful people of The Harry Walker Agency.

Just Ask a Woman is a very personal company, and several terrific women in particular gave it its early life. I will always be grateful to my friends Ruth Ayres, Barrie Dolnick, Ann Skalski, Beth McLure, and Jan Richter for their creativity. Thanks also to Steve Rosenbaum for giving us the space to grow and Holly Koenig for giving us the connections to expand.

Listening to women takes an open heart, an assessing mind, and the willingness to let intuition run wild alongside discipline. To Just Ask a Woman's Kelsey MacMillan and Tracy Brogan, who kept me honest and on track through the writing of this book, I owe so many thanks. I am indebted also to Jen Levine, the first person I hired at Just Ask a Woman; she is not only the managing director who created the philosophy of marketing *with* women but also an extraordinary thinker whose insights and contributions to this book are immeasurable. I could not have done this without her.

I also send a special thank you to the 3,000 women and counting who shared their heartfelt thoughts with me, as well as to the hundreds of women—girlfriends, colleagues, role models, and mentors—who taught me the true power of women in the marketplace and in the world.

Finally, I wish to thank the people who have been my personal lifeline, not just through the process of writing this book, but always. When people ask me, "Why do you seem so happy?" I say, "Because I am lucky to have a family that loves me." To my brother, Jack Finlayson, and my parents, Mary and Ray Finlayson, who have believed in me and made me want to make them proud, I send my love. And to my husband Joe—the light of my life, who was there for the late trips home from the road, the weekends at the computer, and the crazy everyday challenges of being married to a working woman for nearly 25 years—thank you for your love and your partnership. And a pat on the head to my writing companion DannyBoy, a little dog with a heart of gold.

To all of these wonderful friends and allies, I will always be grateful.

INTRODUCTION

This book is for all the marketers who are trying to win with their most powerful customer: women. You probably know just how powerful they are. Although women comprise 51.4 percent of the U.S. population, they buy or influence the purchase of 85 percent of all products and services.[1] Their purchasing dominance and demands on you will only increase with their rising wealth, education, independence, and longevity. Today, women earn $1 trillion annually.[2] For decades, female consumers have driven all the obvious categories of food and beauty and household products. Now they make 80 percent of all health care choices, purchase 65 percent of all new cars, and comprise 50 percent of the traveling population.[3] Women are booting up the computers, remodeling the homes, investing the money, and making more decisions on everything from real estate to telecommunications. And there's no turning back.

In addition to the avalanche of statistics, you may have also heard that women expect to be marketed to differently. In other words, they want to be considered special. Why? What does that mean? Do they want different products than men want? Do they want you to feminize your advertising? What are the benefits if you get it right? What are the costs if you get it wrong? What can you do about it?

Just Ask a Woman is for any marketer who is puzzled by or frustrated about how to respond to the enormity of this undeniable, business-transforming female influence. This book will answer your questions with real-world, practical, and actionable strategies to build your business with women.

This book is the result of my career of listening to women, not only through my marketing consultancy, Just Ask a Woman, but also from my 20 years in advertising, marketing, and communications for some of America's and the world's best known brands. I have walked in your shoes, both as a marketer and as a CEO. I hope that by reading this book, you will think differently about your most important customer. Perhaps you will soon agree with Procter & Gamble chairman and CEO A. G. Lafley, who summed it up for me this way: "The people who buy our products aren't 'consumers.' They're women. It's all about getting to know these women personally." This book is your chance to get to know women personally. It may change the way you think about your most valuable "consumers."

Your success in the future will not come from marketing to women. That's over. Marketing *to* women means thinking of them as a target, to be sold to or talked at. I believe in marketing *with* women, treating them as business partners and listening to them throughout every step of the marketing process. The greatest marketers are not the best sellers or talkers. They are the best listeners.

However, with the pressures of quarterly earnings, rising competition, and even your best intentions, it can be difficult to listen personally to what women want. Let *Just Ask a Woman* do some of it for you.

I Love to Listen

I am an inveterate eavesdropper, observer, and listener. I learned it from my mom. She could get anyone to open up, from the waitress in a diner to the head of a department store. I inherited her gift and honed the skill as a marketer. When others talk, I watch for the subliminal signals, the body language and the unspoken intentions. And because I like to listen, women easily confide in me. I am honestly fascinated with them as human beings and as consumers.

In 1999 I founded Just Ask a Woman, a marketing consultancy dedicated to understanding what women want and why they buy. As corny as it may sound, when I started the company, I wrote this mission on a paper napkin: to be the most compelling interpreter of women's voices in the marketplace.

Just Ask a Woman is the most recent evolution of a career that has spanned several different worlds, all of them revolving around women. I spent the first three years of my career in Philadelphia, working in communications for my alma mater, Saint Joseph's University. What did that have to do with women? In 1970 Saint Joe's admitted women full-time, after 120 years of being all male. As one of the first female graduates, and later as the college's public relations director, I helped convert the school's image from an all-boys college to a coeducational liberal arts university.

I moved to New York in 1978 when I married my husband Joe, and I began a 10-year climb at one of the world's foremost companies for women, Avon Products Inc. During the 1980s Avon was still coming to grips with a changing society in which working women were no longer home when the Avon lady rang the doorbell. As director of motivational communications to the 500,000 Avon representatives, I learned what women around the country were feeling about their burgeoning independence and financial power. Later, as director of advertising for the company's U.S. business, I discovered the landmines and victories of selling to women the way they wanted to be sold to. Our pitch then was as much about confidence and opportunity as it was about lipstick.

It is interesting to contrast those early stirrings of female power at Avon in the 1980s with the words of the company's current chairman and CEO, Andrea Jung. I worked with Andrea throughout the late 1990s as her advertising partner and was proud to witness the development of what she now calls the "company for women." Andrea explains the growth of women's consumer power today this way: "We are in 143 countries, and I have the privilege and luxury of watching what I would consider the evolution of women in society. It's in various stages in different parts of the world. We are on the verge, from a consumer point of view, of women being in power, being financially independent and driving the brand decisions. We are so close to it. This is the moment for the companies that understand that."

In 1989 I left Avon to build a career in the advertising agency business. At both Ally & Gargano advertising and DDBNeedham New York, I was the most senior woman—and the only woman on the office management boards. Being called the youngest, the first, and the only woman was a badge of honor, and I tried to take the responsibility of role model seriously. In an ironic early career moment at DDBNeedham, I remember asking if I could join the new business pitch for the Maidenform lingerie account, not only because I was a woman, but also because I wore the product. The decision was made to involve only the agency leadership, which at the time was all male. The sight of six men sitting in a conference room, picking up lacy underwear and analyzing it, is frozen in my memory. (No, they did not win that account.) During my years at DDBNeedham, however, with clients like Johnson & Johnson skin care, James River paper products, Seiko watches, and Clairol hair coloring, women and their lives became the focus of my days.

In 1994 I joined N. W. Ayer & Partners, first as president of the New York office, and one year later as the first female CEO of what was the first agency in the United States. Our clients included AT&T, Procter & Gamble, Avon, Continental Airlines, and KitchenAid. That job kept my eyes on female consumers, as well as on the agency's bottom line. In the role of CEO I gained my greatest empathy for marketers, who spend every day in the hot seat and make the tough calls, while trying always to remember the importance of customers.

I also grew to appreciate the key roles of women in marketing and communications. I was honored with the two biggest awards for women in advertising: Advertising Women of New York's Advertising Woman of the Year in 1995 and New York Women in Communications' Matrix Award for Advertising in 1997. The Matrix Award, given to women like Meryl Streep for film and Katharine Graham for newspapers, was especially rewarding because it was linked not only to achievement but also to personal leadership of other women.

Over those years, marketing techniques grew more sophisticated, but one thing did not change much: the way companies listened to women. It is hard to believe that every day in the United States, women in big cities and small towns walk into focus groups, the warhorses of research, to share their opinions with the marketers who want their business (and to make a quick $50).

The F Word

If you have not been to a focus group in a while, here is a quick refresher. Women are recruited based on their demographics and their answers to questions like "Does your family eat peanut butter?" "Do you worry about your health?" and "Is your pet the center of your life?" If they answer correctly, women are invited to come to a focus group.

About eight to ten women show up at a dreary building in a

nondescript strip mall, fill in more answers on a clipboard, and warily eye the other women in the waiting room. Eventually, they file back to a windowless, fluorescent-lit room (the most un-flattering lighting for women, by the way) to sit in hard chairs at a Formica conference table adorned with cans of warm soda and bowls of stale chips. A moderator who is probably tired from completing earlier groups on deodorants or insurance greets them. She invites them to relax for a casual conversation about a subject such as incontinence with the following caveats. She professes to have nothing to do with the ideas that they are about to discuss, and she reveals that the room is bugged with hidden recording devices and that a two-way mirror conceals other people who are watching, even though the women cannot see them.

Thankfully, the women cannot see the room behind the mir-ror. Unlike the focus group room, the darkened observation room looks like the command center from Star Trek. Clients and agency partners are seated in cushy armchairs. A refrigerator is stocked with every sort of drink. Servers solicit food orders for the preference of the clients, unless the gourmet lasagna is al-ready on the way. Although they have been through this drill dozens of times, there is a buzz among the backroom crowd, like a kind of market research reunion.

What are they talking about? They talk about the women in the focus group room, how they look and whether they are really *their* customers. (I have noticed that the unattractive women are generally suspected to be noncustomers.) For the most part, they are not listening to the focus group's conversation being piped in. They are talking to each other about their ideas, their next meet-ings, and movies they have seen recently.

Meanwhile, in the focus group room, the women are making the best of a bad situation. The moderator (whose style often bears a striking resemblance to your third grade teacher in the way that she belabors the simplest questions) is focusing on the most opinionated woman in the room. Every focus group has one person who rules the group. She is the woman who is an authority on everything, whether tropical diseases or the importance of calcium in fig cookies. The rest of the women start silently to strategize over how they can take her out because she is such a takeover queen, and the shy women shrink into their skins, casting furtive looks in the mirror, wishing they had put on some lipstick before they came.

For two hours, women drag their way through the linear questions until at last the clock nears the closing minutes, and you can see them start to pick up their purses and prepare to get the money and run. By then the folks in the back room are out the door, giving each other high fives if one of their ideas survived and discussing their next status meeting.

Now, this is a very harsh take on focus groups. Certainly, there are great moderators who make the groups fun, stimulating, and productive. Sometimes, good insights can result. But from 20 years behind the two-way mirror, and from countless discussions with marketing colleagues, I believe that this nightmare description has a lot of truth in it.

The Price of Bad Listening

Why does this matter? This low-grade listening may be how you get information that guides your company's decisions. Often, this qualitative work is used to direct hugely expensive quantitative studies, judge creative work, or inspire new product ideas. Marketers are not the only ones listening this way. America's presidential candidates count on focus groups to frame their communications platforms.

This is frightening for two reasons. In today's competitive environment, the stakes are too high to depend on this surrogate for listening. In addition, beyond the format, realize that the quality of the listening is contingent on the quality of the listener. To whom are you delegating your customer listening? How are you treating the customer who pays your paycheck?

Bad listening is such a loss. Women are the most amazing thinkers and creative problem solvers. The lost opportunity of getting their best insights is the biggest price of all.

Over the past three years at Just Ask a Woman, 3,000 women have talked to me about their lives because I listen to women the way they like to talk. Have you ever watched or been part of a group of women in a restaurant or at a hair salon? Women are natural bonders, easily sharing the most personal feelings, even if they just met. Women like to share what is on their minds, particularly if it is a problem.

That is why women are dumbfounded when marketers do not listen to them. Women feel like they are giving out all the right signals about what they want. That is why, when they see so many oddball products and bad services, their response is an incredulous, "Are you talking to *me?*"

At Just Ask a Woman, we never do focus groups. We listen to women in environments that are informal yet energized. We invite 25 women (the bigger crowd affords less pressure and more participation) into an elegant hotel meeting room that is set up to resemble a TV talk show format. For two hours, with cameras *and* clients in the room with us, we hustle to ask and listen with just one powerful tool: a microphone. The women feel like their opinions matter. We respond when they change the subject. We pursue seemingly tangential remarks because they often lead to surprising revelations. Women shake our hands and thank us when they leave (some even hug us goodbye) because someone finally listened.

We also listen to women in smaller groups and one-on-one

conversations through in-home, filmed DocuDiaries. No matter what the venue, the method of operating is the same. Women are smart. Women are important. As marketers, our role is to listen. And our marketing clients listen right alongside us, face to face with their own consumers. No two-way mirror separates our marketers from the women who sign their paychecks.

This book can be your way of coming face to face with women's voices. You can channel the most comprehensive realities of women's lives directly to your brand—just as if you had done all this listening yourself.

At this point, I would like to take a moment to address male and female readers separately.

The Guy/Girl Thing

This may be a gross generalization, but if you are a man, you might be feeling confused and a little irritated about this subject—confused because for a couple of decades or more, the women you work with (and probably the women in your personal life) have insisted, "We can do anything men can do," "Pay us the same salary," "We want the same things," and "We're no different from guys."

You also might be irritated because you have heard your female consumers and employees demanding that you "treat us the same, but understand our unique needs." In other words, women seem to want different and individualized treatment. You might feel that you have already evolved into the most politically correct person you can be. You are trying to do the right things. Your ads are not offensive; your products keep improving; and you keep upping the customer service ante. You are not insulting women. Enough already. Why bother going any further? If for no other reason, consider your bottom line.

I know that men listen, but they listen differently. This next story may seem to be a generalization about men, but consider this example.

My husband Joe and I are friends with Paul, a young guy who married Amy about two years ago and then oddly seemed to show up alone all the time. We both kept wondering, "What's up with Paul? Is something wrong between him and Amy?" Finally, Joe went out to dinner with Paul, and when he came home, I asked, "Well? What's happening?" And Joe answered, "I don't know. I never asked." "You *never asked?*" I shrieked. I couldn't believe it. If the tables were turned, a female friend would have poured her heart out. Women like to talk, especially when something bothers them. Male readers of this book might reevaluate women's passion to share as a talent for market espionage.

By the way, you might also be the kind of guy who is wondering what women want in your personal life. This book might be a real eye-opener that can help you in that area, too.

If you are a female marketer or sales leader, you may be feeling something entirely different about this focus on women. You have worked like a dog to get where you are. You have succeeded by telling it straight and by doing the job. You have done it by showing that you are no different from men. You are not in your job to work as a female advocate or to fulfill some quota. You are a businessperson. You have made it alongside men, and you are not responsible for all the women in the world. As one high-ranking woman in a financial services company boasted to me, "Whenever I speak here, it's as a professional. Never as a woman."

Here is a hard reality for the men and women who read this book. Understanding the language and needs of female consumers would be a lot easier if the women in business felt comfortable sharing their own insights as women. Unfortunately, many female executives maintain their own codes of silence because they cannot or will not risk their hard-won positions. Exposing their intuition risks embarrassment and diminishment, so they stay quiet for the most part when the subject of the unique needs of female consumers comes up: Don't ask, don't tell.

At its extreme, this is a case of women turning into what I call *minimen*. Many of them have left their female intuition and experience outside the office for too long and refuse even to acknowledge that women can bring unique traits and talents to the marketing and selling scene. What starts as a defense against possible discrimination can grow into a permanent shutdown that is a real personal loss for these women—and a professional loss for the marketing process.

Thousands of women have decided just to keep their feelings and insights as women separate from their business lives. It is a call that they make, just as some men do. Here are two examples.

I am often invited to lead internal company brainstorms on women's issues. In one of these sessions, the men were expounding about how much easier today's moms have it. The women at the table squirmed and remained silent. Later, several women confessed that they wished that the men had not been in the room because the women worried that sharing their own experiences as working moms would have diminished their stature in their male colleagues' eyes. One female executive acknowledged, "It was better to keep quiet. I could never deal with their comments about my life issues."

Second, during an internal audit intended to launch a women's marketing program for a major health services company, the company boasted that it really valued the participation of many senior women in its business. I was asked to interview several of these women to learn about the virtues of the company's policies. After trying to reach one overscheduled and harried woman several times, I finally caught her on her car phone during her late-night commute. I asked her, "Is this a good company for women?" "Is this a good company for women?" she repeated. "If you don't have a husband, a child, friends, a plant, or a life. Oh yeah, it's a great company for women." The next day, she was back to business as usual.

In these and many other cases, the women who could be the best sources of information on the needs of female customers are shutting down and just keeping on. Meanwhile, as the corporate code of silence or ignorance rolls on, female buying power continues to become the biggest market force in the United States. The price for this Mars/Venus problem is paid in the marketplace, where, for these very human reasons, companies continue to underdeliver to their most important audience.

Here is what's at stake. As long as marketers, salespeople, and communicators work with old or obvious insights about women, they will struggle to claim their fair share of women's dollars. Recently, a senior male director in a Fortune 100 corporation said to an audience, "Our competitors aren't making any great strides with women, so what's our competitive advantage in trying?" Why try? It is a matter of winning. Or not.

Just because women are the leading consumer group does not mean that those who want women's dollars or share of mind can wait for women to come to their door. Women watch. Women compare. Women choose. Which competitor will be the one to create the innovation that will change women's buying habits? How do you speak to a woman in a way that makes her switch brands? Who will get her loyalty and keep it? And who will lose it, without even knowing it was happening? *Just Ask a Woman* has the answers.

This book will take on some of the most frustrating problems that women hit you with. Why do women buy what they do? Why do they fall out of love with one brand and adopt a new one? Why do they say one thing but mean another? Why do they take so long to make decisions? Why do they want so much attention at the same time that they want to be left alone? Why do they get so wrapped up in details? Why do they take things personally? How do you sell to her without *selling* her? What, in sum, do women want?

Women as the Go-To Problem Solvers

Department stores are in a tailspin right now. Shoppers are flocking to mass outlets that have figured out how to improve quality and service while maintaining low prices. Boutiques, online, and even chain fashion stores are skimming the cream from the market. This has left store managers scratching their heads and wondering, "Where are the shoppers?" That is the wrong question. The right one is, "Where are the *women*?"

Yet if you suggested to the leaders of many retail stores that they ought to learn more about what women want, they would likely say, "Oh, we already know about them." But why don't stores listen? Why don't they change? Why don't they succeed?

The automotive industry has also had a slow learning curve relative to women. Women are buying more cars than are men. However, the reason is not that the sellers have made many advances to understand them. It is that women have figured out how to go around the system by doing as much research and investigation in advance of that first visit to the showroom.

The list goes on and on to include pharmaceutical companies that rely on women as the caregivers and financial services companies that are finally recognizing her power, as well as technology, home improvement, the travel industry, entertainment, and even the female bastions of beauty, food, children, and family products. There isn't a business today that does not rely on women to make or break its brand.

This book is meant to help you market, sell, and connect

more effectively with women, and it is designed to be digestible enough that it will not add to the already high anxiety of your daily work but will still deliver women's truths.

About This Book

Just Ask a Woman will do for you what you would do if you had the time. It will decode what female consumers want so that it is no longer an irritating, frustrating mystery. The insights are continually tied to practical "now what?" action. Here is how this book works:

Chapter 1 is a checkup for you as a marketer. Just in case you think that you already know everything there is to know about women, try this reality check on your female IQ. This chapter will help you as marketers understand whether you are listening.

The next seven chapters capture the areas that galvanized the women I interviewed, no matter what their age, income, education, or lifestyle. Each chapter has critical lessons for marketers in nearly every category, distilled into five ways to crack the code with women.

Chapter 2 is about the mother-lode issue that drives all the rest of the chapters: women's stress and the effect it has on them as consumers. You will learn about the stress filter that she places on every decision she makes and about how you can anticipate her feelings by not competing with her stress.

Chapter 3 tackles what might be one of your greatest frustrations: Why do women take so long to decide? How does a woman make up her mind about my brand? You will walk through her decision quadrant, four powerful variables that make her say yes or no to you.

Chapter 4 takes you shopping, her style. *Vigilante shopper* is the description of a woman on a mission who has been burned and is taking no prisoners in her search for the value and service that she demands. You see who gets it and who doesn't get it.

Chapter 5 tackles the inner/outer beauty conundrum. Why do women say that they only care about what is inside yet obsess about how they look? What does this mean to you when a woman sees the way you look at her?

Chapter 6 touches on a subject that women bring up in every interview: technology. If you understand women's love-hate affair with technology, you are likely to have a satisfied customer online or on the line. Otherwise, brace yourself for "cancel" or a resounding slam of the phone. You will find ways to humanize the automation.

Chapter 7 is the guide for anyone in a business in which personal relationships are involved in the transaction with women. In this chapter you will hear women tell the stories of what is happening when the stakes are high and what you can do about it.

Chapter 8 describes women's ultimate fantasy: being nurtured, renewed, and restored. Can your brand cash in on this craving, or are you one of the reasons she needs to escape?

The last chapter is a blueprint for how you can change from a marketer who sells to a listener who wins.

Throughout the book you will hear stories from the thousands of women I have interviewed. You will hear women's voices in their own words, unvarnished and passionate. Identities and everything proprietary to particular clients are protected, but you will feel the force of what they want. Their needs will be translated into ideas that you can use.

You will also hear the voices of 19 CEOs and marketing executives, many of them arguably the most successful marketers to women. They will share their struggles and the lessons that they learned while facing the same challenges that you do. In addition to A. G. Lafley of Procter & Gamble and Andrea Jung of Avon, you will hear from Christina Johnson, CEO of Saks Fifth Avenue; Paul Higham, former chief marketing officer of Wal-Mart; Dan Brestle, president of Estee Lauder; Lisa Caputo, president of the Women & Co. division of Citigroup; Cathie Black, president of Hearst Magazines; Andrea Alstrup, corporate vice president of Johnson & Johnson; and many others. They will share ideas that work and their best advice on how to help ensure that women choose your brand.

In addition, I will share my own experiences, successes, and lessons from my career and my life. I have always believed in bringing my self as a woman to work. My comfort with using my head and my heart makes this a very personal book.

I wrote this book for two reasons. First, I wrote it for you, the marketers, salespeople, communicators, and businesspeople who make it happen. I was and still am one of you. I want you to be more successful with women.

And I wrote it for the women. At the end of every session, I ask, "What should companies always do and never do to get your business?" Women share their best ideas but often say, "Mary Lou, will they ever listen to us?" I always promise them that you will. This book is keeping that promise.

Keeping the Promise

I promised that this book would include the unvarnished words of women in order to reveal the truths of your most important customers. I will close this introduction with words from one of them. Here's her truth: "I think the main thing with every woman in America is that we don't want to feel pressured to have to buy anything. We feel pressure from our husbands. We feel pressure from our kids. Some of us don't even get to go to the bathroom by ourselves. If we want to buy something, it had better be easy." What is her advice for marketers? "Always respect women as intelligent consumers. We don't want product shoved down our throats. We want options to think about it later or to shop for a better price. We don't want to be manipulated. We want interaction so we can give feedback for better products and services."

Just Ask a Woman is their chance to talk to you. It is also your chance to listen and get answers on the most powerful consumer of this century. Get ready to crack to the code of what women want.

CHAPTER 1

A Checkup
for Marketers:
Listening or Not?

We already know about women.

Successful marketers are usually good listeners, but today's competitive environment calls for more refined listening skills, particularly when your primary customers are women. Staying current with women's needs can be a challenge, though, because of their increasing levels of education, income, independence, and networking. In addition, there are so many different segments of women, each complex and evolving, which makes the listening job even more demanding.

As a marketer, you may feel that you already understand women. Perhaps you feel that a customer is a customer and that your experience with male customers prepares you for understanding women. I have worked with some clients in whom I could feel the hesitancy to embrace the idea of women as the target consumer. I have heard this expressed in many ways: "Won't that limit us?" "Men won't want our products if women are the main focus," and "We don't want to turn this into a women's company."

Let's say that your brand is accepted and used by women. On one hand, your success may cause you to wonder why you need to read this book because you seem to be doing OK with female customers. On the other hand, perhaps you have observed some organizational and cultural roadblocks that keep your organization from truly listening to women. Perhaps your traditional processes, whether in marketing, sales, or product development, are somehow shortcutting your stream of needed consumer insights.

How can you tell if your company is really listening to women? The following is a checkup for marketers: 10 of the listening roadblocks I have heard most often in my marketing career. Are any of them familiar to you?

A Listening Checkup

Read the following 10 statements. Think of this as a listening reality check. If you have ever said or heard your marketing, sales, or account team say one of the following, you may not be truly listening to women.

1. "Oh, they *always say that.*"

They means women, and the dismissive pronoun is already a clue to a lack of customer respect. You may hear your team say this to the complaints that female customers raise. It is a signal that your team may have stopped listening to women and that they still have not fixed what could be a chronic problem for your business. This attitude can distance marketers from women. This first statement is often heard in the back room at focus groups. In fact, the dynamic of focus groups can instigate the problem.

Behind the two-way mirror in the focus group room, marketers are literally separated from consumers. Isolated in their hidden, cushioned armchairs, marketers are watching, not interacting with consumers. Like scientists observing the way lab rats respond to stimuli, the back room tends to scrutinize female consumers as if they were subjects in an experiment. Rather than engage with women, marketers and agency folks talk to each other behind the mirror and too often react to women's negative feedback with sarcastic eye rolls and bored head nods. So, rather than help marketers stay open to listen for what women really mean, the focus group format drives distanced *non*learning—which is a dangerous way to get market intelligence.

Have you ever sat in the same room as consumers? You undoubtedly have seen the dismissive attitudes evaporate when the respectful listening kicks in.

2. *"We did some groups with women a while ago."*

This is code for "we held about three focus groups in Paramus in 1998, and we are still relying on the opinions of those 24 women." This attitude assumes that women do not change and that asking them once is enough. It also assumes that the focus groups were recruited properly and moderated well. How many times have you attended a dud focus group? Is that impression ever noted on the focus group report? In my experience, poor groups are forgotten as soon as the client and agency cars leave the parking lot. However, a written report on an unsuccessful group can live on in files as truth. What if those are the groups on which you are relying to make important decisions? Women are constantly evolving and reevaluating what your company's products mean to them in the context of their lives. Old learning is almost as bad as no learning.

For future reference, you might ask attendees to include a

note on the qualitative reports that indicates their satisfaction with the findings and their assessment of the quality of the work.

3. "Women say that, but they don't really mean it."

I have often heard this defensive comment from ad agency creative teams that do not agree with what women say. Sometimes, this statement is true on the surface. For instance, when women say they want to see "real" women in skin care ads, they mean it and they don't. What they do mean is that they want to see likable human beings in ads rather than perfect automatons. What they do not mean is that they want to see unattractive models with bad or average skin representing a highly effective skin care cream. Accepting or dismissing women's comments outright is a mistake.

A smart moderator is prepared for the rote answers of your category. If you ask a woman, "Do you really mean that?" she will clarify for you. Women also welcome the respectful moderator who says, "Maybe I'm just being a devil's advocate, but even though you just said you want to see real women, earlier you said that this pretty ad was appealing. Could you explain why?" She will. She is watching to see if you are paying attention, and if you let her off the hook, she is unlikely to bother to correct your misperception.

4. "The customer service department handles complaints when women call in."

Customer service departments are as good as the leadership that drives them and the brand philosophy that inspires them. Great ones build customer loyalty and function as effective listening vehicles. Sometimes, however, these departments are trained and compensated as if they occupied the lowest rung on the marketing ladder. In other words, your first line of listening may be delegated to a group, who though schooled in the scripts of your company's answers may be one of your lowest paid, highest turnover departments. These folks can get pretty weary of hearing repeated complaints, and they eventually burn out, shut down, check off the communications report, and go home to get a good night's sleep. Some systems have a recording stating that the call will be monitored for service quality. However, have you ever had a supervisor interrupt a bad customer service call while you were on it? If you have not sat with your customer service team and tried out the system yourself in over six months, you may not discover a critical leak in your listening network—and you risk being out of the loop as a listener yourself.

At Just Ask a Woman, we created the Collective, a database of the women we have interviewed in person. Even though we are always on the street and in the market listening to women, we also e-mail these "alumnae" frequently to keep a reality check on what women are thinking, especially in relation to current events. Their long and deep responses are like our own customer care department and serve as valuable checks on our own theories. For example, our alumnae predicted the weak fourth-quarter retail results of 2002. In June of that year we asked them, "What did you learn about shopping this summer?" They bragged that the economic downturn had taught them to curb spending, research sale prices, and postpone their near- and midterm needs.

5. *"Women will say they want the world if you ask them, but we can't afford to respond to every little thing they ask for."*

No, you can't. On the other hand, some of women's requests are make-or-break issues. For instance, in the car buying business, women have been saying for years that they resent male car dealers referring all their attention to their husbands or ignoring them when they shop alone. For a long time, women just felt irritated or tolerated the behavior. Today, many women have devised strategies to avoid time in the dealership. Instead, they do research online and make decisions in advance of visiting the showroom. In this case, what might have seemed like trifles built until women took matters into their own hands.

As a marketer, it is up to you to call the shots on whether it is profitable to respond to women's needs. But the first step is to listen so that you can gauge just how seriously she means what she is saying to you.

6. "Women don't know what they want; we need to lead them where they really want to go."

I often hear this kind of comment in the fashion, beauty, and design areas. It is a we-know-better attitude that is a blend of egotistical artistry and insecurity. Certainly, many women look to these industries for inspiration and advice, and they want the style community to project what is next. But when the lack of listening among designers results in racks of unsold fads or empty retail stores, it is evident that women do know better. The trick is to ask women not what to design but, "What do you prefer to wear?" or "What makes you feel comfortable or pretty?" In other words, ask women, "What makes you happy?" instead of "What should I design for you?"

7. "Women could never understand the complexities of our business like we do."

This is the kind of trap that the health and finance companies fall into. Although all female patients do not have medical degrees or MBAs from Stanford, they do know plenty about their health and their money. Most women are willing to admit what they do not know, so they do their homework, conduct research online, and check their boards of directors. Be watchful if your communications complicate rather than simplify. Be careful if your sales force feels smart because they can out-lingo the customer. She will find someone else who speaks her language.

To help your service and sales force become better listeners, encourage them to invite women to talk first. Ask open-ended questions that allow her to be in charge, such as "Tell me about your life," "What's the best health care relationship you've had?" or "What would be an ideal way for you to receive communications from me in the future?" She will set the rules, her style.

8. "She's too young (or too old, too fat, too dull, etc.) to be our customer."

Most marketers would not say this aloud, but I have heard it whispered many, many times. Unfortunately, some marketers like to think of their customers as people they would invite to a cocktail party in their homes. Look at the profile of your customer target on your marketing strategies. So often, the ideal customer is described as young, attractive, ambitious, bright, and confident. Rarely does a strategy define a brand's customers as unattractive, uneducated, or satisfied with the status quo. Here is a simple test: Walk down a busy street. How many supermodels and Rhodes scholars walk by? Are there enough on which to build a big business? Love the customer you have, or she will fall in love with someone else.

9. "This new product improvement isn't exactly what women asked for; it's just slightly more complicated (or takes a little longer to work, takes some getting used to, etc.)."

Marketers who disregard women's needs for simplifying, saving time, and maintaining control are making a big mistake. Women generally ask for simple, practical things. A woman wants cleaning products without harsh chemicals. She wants a cell phone with number buttons she can read without glasses. She wants a human on the other end of the customer line when she calls, instead of entering the phone tree maze. The genius of new product development is responding to what women really want while delighting them with easier assembly, faster results, or more intuitive usage. The success of the lightweight Sony VAIO laptop and Listerine's fast-acting Cool Strips testifies to this. Listening to women will lead you to simpler, and ideally more successful, products.

10. "Oh yes, we listen to women. We even have a special women's department devoted to figuring out what they want."

This statement is the most worrisome of all. On the contrary, it might make more sense for some companies to create a special department to figure out what the male minority wants and apply the lion's share of their marketing, communications, and sales resources to the customer majority. Delegating listening to women to a special department might jumpstart the internal focus on female customers. More often than not, however, special initiatives degenerate into an excuse to marginalize the economic clout of women. Then, when it comes to yearly financial allocations, it is an easy budget line to cut.

There is an underlying problem with delegating the task of listening to women to a few specialists. That decision lets the other marketing, sales, and service employees off the hook for understanding women themselves. Listening to the leading customer group is everyone's job.

Time to Listen

If you have heard or said just one or two of these statements, it's time to take a fresh look at how your organization listens to women. Marketing with women is about more than selling them what you make. It is about understanding the most powerful feelings and truths in women's lives so that you will discover the kind of insights that lead to competitive ideas. That is where you will find the answers to how she makes decisions, why she buys, and what makes her loyal to you.

The next seven chapters decode the most compelling issues on the minds of today's female consumers. Chapter 2 deals with the most overriding theme I have heard from the thousands of women whom I have interviewed: the stress in their lives. See how it affects their feelings about your brand.

Self-Induced Stress

I go to bed tired, and I wake up tired.

I'm not a psychotherapist, but over the past three years I have often felt like one. During that time, 3,000 women confided their feelings to me. I listened to these women in my role as CEO of Just Ask a Woman, a strategic marketing company I founded in 1999 to understand what women want and why they buy. This is no small task. Women buy or influence the purchase of 85 percent or more of what is sold,[1] making them truly the most powerful consumers of our time. Major corporations like General Motors, Citigroup, Johnson & Johnson, Estee Lauder, and Lifetime Television have hired me to find out what women wanted from their brands. As a kind of brand therapist, I interpreted women's truths into product, communications, service, and marketing solutions for them and for dozens of Fortune 500 companies. I will reveal the greatest lessons I have learned from listening to women so that you can leverage this learning to market with women successfully.

This book focuses on the seven most compelling themes I heard from women. This chapter addresses the number-one issue that influences all the others: stress. Women's feelings about stress in their lives threaded through every one of the 3,000 conversations. This chapter is not just about how stressed they are. You may know that already. It is about why different segments of women are stressed and how their stress affects your brand's success. In addition, this chapter lays the groundwork for the rest of the book because you will see that a woman's stress filter drives the way she decides, shops, and behaves.

Why? Thanks to their ability to live multiple lives as employees, daughters, wives, moms, and friends, women are shoving and squeezing more into every morning, noon, and night to create seemingly 25-hour days. Women prize their bottomless capacity to do more. However, the resulting stress is killing them. Many women have given up on the dreaded B word (balance) and would settle for one sane day at a time.

Let me guess what might be going through your mind as you read this: "My life is stressed, too. I'm barely able to keep up with all the responsibilities and commitments in my life, so why should I feel bad about my female customers?" Admit it. You may even be thinking that your stress is worse.

It is true that the life of a modern marketer is incredibly stressed, but here is a way to understand how women feel. This is not a competition between your stress and hers. While it is helpful to allow your personal reactions to surface, this book is your customer's turn to be heard. As a marketer, unless you can open your mind and empathize with what she feels, you will keep frustrating her and losing her business. To gain her as a customer, first understand how to destress her life as a woman. The stress contest is not one that you would want to win anyway.

Lesson 1. Accept Her Stress; Don't Compete with It

When I speak about women's lives and particularly their stress, two things inevitably happen. When I walk offstage to meet the audience, the men say, "Why are they all so stressed?" Then they add, "My wife always says exactly what you just said." I answer, "Then why aren't you listening to your wife?" In contrast, when I stop in a ladies' room to freshen up after a speech, the women there turn to me and say, "Thank you for telling the truth. That's just the way we feel." And I wonder, "Why don't they tell their colleagues and bosses instead of me?" Whether you are a man or a woman, the answers to how stressed women feel—as consumers and as human beings—are right in your midst. By listening to the stress that women experience with your business, you can avoid service and product pitfalls so that they choose you and stay with you as a customer.

Why does it matter whether companies understand women's stress? Like it or not, stress is standing between you and your marketing success with women. Its effects pervade every decision women make about your business, whether it is finance, beauty,

---

ADVICE ON CREATING A LISTENING CULTURE

"I believe that the company has always been supportive of women, but obviously 15 to 20 years ago, it was much more male. The idea that the head of the division can be a woman has been very inspiring to the women who work here. What I have tried to do is to make it a much more user-friendly company. I hear from women all the time that I have been able to make a big difference here in opening up the doors and opening up the windows and letting everybody have an opportunity, both men and women."

—*Cathie Black, president of Hearst Magazines*

technology, health care, entertainment, or retail. You might think that the solution is to figure out how to sell more to women to alleviate the stress. However, the real question for a marketer is, How can you even begin to connect effectively with women if their stress gets in the way? Remember that if you don't make the connection, you don't make the sale. If your product contributes to her stress because it is complicated or undependable, she will select one of the many competitive choices available to her.

I will start by cracking the code on stress by life stage (from teens to young adults, from moms to empty nesters), and then I will connect it to how she sees and buys your brand. In later chapters I will decipher the effect of stress on her decision making, her shopping, and her receptivity to your communications.

Just How Stressed Is She?

To understand the nature of stress, I have asked many women to describe a typical day. Usually, the pressure begins very early and does not end until the woman passes out at night. Consider this example:

> I'm up at 5:45 A.M. I wake the kids and start the breakfast downstairs. I'm back upstairs to get the baby, pass the kids' rooms again to wake them AGAIN, feed the baby, get the kids dressed, get in the car and drive to the day care center across town to drop off the baby, head in the opposite direction to take the kids to school, then get to my office by 8:15. I work pretty much through lunch, and then around 4, I reverse my trip to pick everybody up, head home, and start some kind of dinner. After dinner, I help the kids with their homework, put the baby to bed, nag the kids to go to bed a million times, and then try to do a little of my own homework because I am taking some courses on the side. When it gets late, I walk around the house in the dark, picking up stuff to throw in the

washer, and sometimes I go online for a couple of minutes, until I crash into bed around 1 A.M. And then I wake up and do it all over again.

It is amazing that this woman even had time to talk to me. Hers is not an unusual story. Imagine placing your product and your ad messages into the middle of that day.

Surprisingly, while many marketers might believe that there are huge differences between the testimonials of busy moms and those of their teenage and college-age daughters, they actually share many of the same worries and desires.

Stress in Training

The first time I heard an 18-year-old complain that she was stressed, it was all I could do to keep my eyes from rolling out of my head. I had to bite my tongue not to shout, "Stress? You want to feel stress? Wait till you're my age and work 12-hour days at a demanding job and have a mortgage and a family and a million things to worry about. Then you'll see what stress is!" I wasn't alone in this reaction. Because our clients are always in the room when I conduct research, I caught the wide-eyed "you've got to be kidding" look on their faces. Had this been a movie, the sound-track would have suddenly stopped for dramatic emphasis.

However, I put aside my personal skepticism and listened to her story. Once I tuned in, I began to detect the strains of stress from young women as early as their mid teens, relating to achievement in school, relationships, and real confusion about what they should be when they grow up. In fact, according to a survey in *USA Today* in August 2000, 74 percent of teenage girls stated that their teen years were more stressful than were those of their parents.[2] (I wonder if their parents would agree.)

Actually, one of the reasons that girls and young women may

be feeling stressed-out and using the language of stress at an early age is that their overwrought, overworked mothers have passed it on to them. These young women are the children of moms who are stretched, exhausted, and certainly stressed.

As a personal example of stress in training, in May 2002 I was invited to speak at Cardinal Dougherty High School, my alma mater in Philadelphia. Because it was a command performance, the entire school population of 1,100 students filed into the auditorium.

I stood on the auditorium stage where once I had been the kid wearing the regulation green uniform and saddle shoes, sitting in the front row, hands neatly folded in my lap. Thirty years later, I felt wiser, but frankly nervous about whether I could connect with these boys and girls. (By the way, do you know just how young 14 looks?) Now, I have spoken to rooms full of CEOs and some pretty scary clients, but looking into the teens' open faces spawned a different kind of fear. They are walking lie detectors.

While there was the usual quota of kids feigning (or actually) sleeping in their seats, most students seemed curious about me. The theme of my talk was the importance of seeking happiness and trying not to fixate on the expectations of others. I spoke about what I had learned through my own career experiences as a CEO, where I felt I could never achieve enough or win enough until I finally quit and started over. The steady stares from the audience made me worry that I had overshot the interest of the teenage crowd.

After I concluded, their enthusiastic reaction amazed me. Sixteen-year-old girls came up to me afterwards and said, "You are describing my life. That's what I'm like in school—I'm so afraid to fail." They translated my story of businesses won and lost into their frustrations with grades and college preparation. One girl said, "Just as you were talking about being stressed, I was staring at my anatomy homework on my lap and worrying if I had it perfect. You were talking about me." Surprisingly, I was telling the stories of *their* lives, not just their parents'.

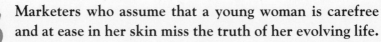 **Marketers who assume that a young woman is carefree and at ease in her skin miss the truth of her evolving life.** An example of a brand that has recognized the stress in young women's lives is Calgon bath products. Once a mainstay of stressed-out older women, the "take me away" theme is now aimed at younger women. On their website, they invite teens to show their school spirit, with contests such as "Calgon High School USA," in which young women can vote for the school with the most team spirit. The website has information on scholarship programs to support their young customers. The company has tied the stress-reducing bath granules to social stress relief for real life. This kind of marketing thinking not only connects with young women but also helps transform a dated brand into a relevant one.

Stress Moves Out on Its Own

Thanks to *Friends* and just about every top-rated sitcom preferred by young consumers, many marketers may believe that women in their 20s are on the top of the world, fresh out of college, enjoying their first jobs, their cool apartments, and their cute boyfriends, while they are partying in bars (on weekdays!). Oh, and by the way, women are thin, happy, and gorgeous with money to spend. Stress? What stress?

That sunny scenario is so untrue for many young women. They feel stress in their careers, their relationships, their finances, and their lives. They are rethinking whether they took the right academic path in college. In fact, many women in their early 20s are still attending college part-time because they have postponed their graduation date because of tuition pressures. They question their career goals and worry about money. They may not have met the love of their lives, and they may still be living at home with Mom and Dad. Ironically, they reminisce about the stress-free days of high school. In May 2001 authors Alexandra Robbins and Abby Wilner coined the phrase *quarterlife crisis* to capture this 20-something anxiety, the essence of which we used to call growing pains.[3]

The unknowns in her life can be overwhelming, and the fears of failing at love, work, and independence are real. In *Working in the Dark,* authors Fawn Fitter and Beth Gulas noted that there are almost 19 million depressed Americans and that depression starts typically in the mid-20s, striking twice as many women as men.[4] It may seem like a big leap from stress to depression, but for many young women, the two may be closely related.

Smart marketers who accept the powerful effects of stress on young women can start to tap their product's role as a stress reliever. A well-known Saturn TV commercial tells the story of a young woman buying her first car. She is stressed about being accepted and making the right decision, and yet is greeted by the dealer's put-downs. Then she goes to the Saturn showroom, where the salesman recognizes her concerns and helps her feel in charge. Although that spot has not run for several years, young women often bring it up to me as a powerfully resonant message. Saturn won with them, not by dwelling on their stress, but by providing a real-world, no-haggle solution and personal respect to compensate for it.

Stress, Another Name for Mom

Unless you are both a marketer and a mom, you may be surprised that many moms look back to their 20s, or their prechild years, as their happiest times. It is not that moms don't love being moms, since many cite motherhood as their greatest pride. However, the stress levels associated with motherhood can be overwhelming. Here is what moms have said to me: "The best time in my life was in my 20s, my early 20s, before children. I was in control then, and it was just me. I could concentrate on what I wanted to do and when I wanted to do it. I have four kids now, and I'm pretty tired and a little bit out of whack." Think about how I just described the 20-somethings. Is this amnesia or revisionist history?

A mother of two agreed: "I feel like I'm going through the trenches right now." Another mom said, "Now that I have three children, I don't get any sleep." Moms often feel overwhelmed and unheard, but some marketers have made them a priority. The Motrin analgesic brand from Johnson & Johnson's McNeil consumer division has repositioned itself to be "Mom's Motrin." For many years, the brand enjoyed success as a product for infants and children, but the company recently recognized the role that the adult ibuprofen product could play as a partner to stressed moms. The commercials promise mothers that, like them, the product fights back against pain, so that Mom can keep on going to take care of her family.

Many moms do persist through stress-filled days, even though they are exhausted. They typically put themselves last after their families, jobs, and even their communities. While there are stay-at-home moms who feel good about their focus and choices, others miss the predictability of the office routine: "I wish I was back at work because clients are easier than kids."

Despite the stress they feel, most moms do not regret their choices regarding their families. At Just Ask a Woman, we created the Collective, which is a database of the women we have interviewed. And in a summer 2002 e-mail survey of 600 women drawn randomly from our group, we asked, "What couldn't you live without?" The number one answer by far was "my husband and children." Motherhood may come with stress, but it also has a healthy helping of joy.

Just ask Carole Black, President of Lifetime Television . . .

Lifetime Television's female-oriented programming made it the number one cable network for all of 2001 and 2002, even above competitors like HBO, ESPN, and VH-1. Carole Black attributes the success to her viewers, many of whom are moms who reward Lifetime with their loyalty. I asked her what she thought women needed in their lives now. "I think that women need to give themselves a break," she replied. "Women sort by others versus sort by self. As a whole, they will always be sensitive about what everyone else is feeling and thinking. It's why women are so delightful to be around—that very thing, of trying to give to everyone and be everything for everyone and be the supermom that maybe their moms were. But maybe their mom didn't have to work as hard—plus they support their parents, their children, and their spouse and friends and do a perfect job at work. No wonder they have no time for themselves. I just wish women would care as much about themselves as they do about everyone else."

As Carole Black noted, more often than not, today's moms are also working in some way outside the home for economic reasons, satisfaction, or both. Note that the U.S. Bureau of the Census reported in 2001 that 55 percent of mothers with children younger than 12 months of age were working.[5]

A March 2002 article in the *New York Times* indicated that the double effect of working and motherhood had driven pregnant women to new levels of schedule management.[6] The article by Linda Villarosa cited a study by the National Institutes of Health that found that the rate of labor inductions had doubled from 1990 to 1998, from 9.5 percent to 19.4 percent of all births. In addition, more than 50 percent of those inductions were elective. As Jun Zhang, the lead investigator of the study, said, "People want to arrange things according to their schedules. We found that the induction rate is highest in December. Everybody wants a Christmas baby, when the relatives are going to be in town." (Talk about accommodating everyone else's needs!)

Another study, conducted by the National Institute of Child Health and Human Development, followed more than 1,000 children in 10 cities over three years. The study examined the effect of mothers who worked 30 hours or more per week by the time their child was 9 months old. Those children achieved weaker school-readiness test scores by age 3 versus the children of mothers who did not work early on.[7] You can imagine how stories like this can drive women's stress through the roof. As a marketer, your awareness of the already heightened sensitivity of working mothers can keep you from developing selling propositions that contribute to their anxiety levels. Thankfully, Wisk detergent's long-time theme of ring around the collar has evolved from its earlier commercials featuring shirts that taunted the laundering mom, which were examples of selling through antagonism, rather than empathy.

With moms feeling all this stress and being so open about it, I feel I ought to acknowledge that I never had children. Although I have listened hard to thousands of moms and am the proud aunt of five nieces and nephews, I cannot claim to have crossed that private line that delineates stress B.C. and A.C. (before children and after children). Instead, and maybe because I had more time to devote to work, my career gets the credit for my stress levels. And although it is a dangerous way to manage, I often found myself thinking of the people who worked for and with me as family, and I lost many nights of sleep worrying about their growth and welfare.

Oddly, when I speak publicly about stress, women ask me whether I have children more often than do men. It is as if I cannot qualify for the condition without kids. I should repeat that stress is not a contest and that there are millions of childfree women who have their own reasons to be stressed, from career to finances to family to health—you name it. Marketers should not forget that either.

The business implications of supporting moms with products and services that respond to their realities and validate their choices are huge. Marketers who insist on showing moms as out-of-control women with bratty kids who mess up the house are feeding that insecurity and ticking the mothers off. Moms are looking for relief and answers, simple and straight. Yet think of all the many commercials for convenience foods that are filmed in fast motion to convey the speed of their lives. A recent commercial for Pledge WipeUps showed a woman dusting in warp speed while the kids watched TV. She does not need to look crazed while she is trying to keep things together and cleaning as the kids veg out. I would not be surprised if some women wonder why the mother does not hand the kids the rag.

Creative marketers find ways to ease moms' stress by taking action instead of talking about it. The folks from J. M. Smucker Company never expected that moms would go for a premade frozen peanut butter and jelly sandwich as a meal for kids. While it might seem easy to make a PB&J sandwich, it is just one more job on Mom's expanded to-do list. The product offers not only convenience but also the added touch of cut-off crusts as a concession to little Sally's preferences. And although the frozen product costs more than handmaking one in the morning, it offers an advantage of freshness because the frozen sandwich does not fully thaw until noon. Despite Smucker's skepticism, after a test in midwestern markets, where the product reeled in $20 million, it is now gaining national distribution.

I would like to make a confession on this one as a marketer and a woman. Remember when I said that stress is not a contest? Well, when I read about these sandwiches, I subverted what I know about today's busy moms and went straight to my own experience. My mom worked throughout all the years that my brother Jack and I were in school. In my prejudiced view, my mom was not "lazy" like these "Smucker mothers." She woke up at 6:30 A.M., made our PB&J sandwiches, and put them in brown bags that Jack and I carried to school. Were they stale at lunchtime? I don't remember whether they were. Were the crusts cut off? No way—there was none of that indulgent stuff in our house. See how my own experience closed me down to the stress of moms today and to a great marketing opportunity? It can happen to all of us. Remember that stress is not a contest and that your personal experiences are not always aligned with those of your female customer.

ADVICE ON SUPPORTING WOMEN

"We recognize that women are largely the decision makers when it comes to the health of the family, and that they are the caregivers, so we have always valued women. We know that women's lives are complicated. So, we have on-site child care facilities for working moms and dads, and programs for balancing work and family, like Lifeworks, an online system for people if they have a problem with child care or elder care or personal health issues."
—*Andrea Alstrup, corporate vice president of Johnson & Johnson*

Lesson 2. Pay Particular Attention to the Needs of Stressed-Out Moms

Mom is the number-one consumer for so many products and services. If you are selling to her, you have the toughest job of all. Can you look at the products you make and figure out how she really uses them with her family? Can you look at where you sell and make the environment more mom and child friendly? How far is your parking lot from the door? How quickly and readily do you respond to her need for infant seats in restaurants, an extra hand on a plane when she travels with a child, a restroom with a changing table that is not right next to the door? (Ever get bumped when you were holding a baby upside down?) If you are operating a customer service line for a mom-centered business, how long do you leave her on hold? Pick up the phone before she picks up and leaves. That holds true for childless women, too.

Stress and the Empty Nester

The older, empty-nest women, whose kids are just packing up for college or moving out (at last!), face different stresses. They still have responsibilities to their children, home, and jobs, coupled with caring for their aging parents. Additionally, they have the stress of health concerns, finances for retirement, and evolving relationships with their spouses. Understand the sources of that newfound stress, or lose them. Women want you to address their intelligence in your advertising, instead of just focusing on their impending menopause and loose bladders. Women are waiting to see if you are going to overlook them. Do they ever appear in your ads? As a marketer, you can bring women front and center in industries where they are your star consumer, such as health care, insurance, luxury goods, and wellness products.

How? Try talking her language. As part of a story I wrote for an April 2002 issue of *MORE*, a magazine devoted to women over 40, I invited five ad agencies to create messages that told marketers about the importance of this segment. One of the most provocative ads was created by DiMassimo Brand Advertising. It featured a straight-to-camera photo of a beautiful 40 something with the line, "If you want my money, stop showing me pictures of my daughter in underwear. And stop pretending you think she's me. That's not 'aspirational.' That's obnoxious. It's your decision." Recognition of that "enough is enough" attitude is rarely seen in advertising to grown-up women.[8]

Think woman, think stress. And then think about what that means when she walks into your store and you do not have what she wants. Think about her reaction when you create a supposedly funny commercial spoofing her hectic life. She does not need you to rub it in that she is stressed. She needs you to get your product or service when, where, and how she wants it. *Now.*

She Is Her Own Worst Enemy

What is ironic about the high stress level of women is that it is self-induced. I do it myself. I had the brilliant idea to throw a party for a large group of high-achieving women in New York on behalf of New York Women in Communications, a professional organization I headed. It was not enough to offer my apartment as the party space and to get the food, flowers, and wine. I had to handwrite the invitations to 200 women, nearly all with personal notes. And I didn't stop there. Two days before the party, I decided to redecorate the living room and the bedroom for the event. I understand what it means to create your own stress.

When women are asked about their days, they will tell stories like the previous, indicating how much they are flooded with the needs of others. It is not about being a martyr. It is her female machismo kicking in, showing that she can do it all.

In the Lifetime Report on Women, a qualitative and quantitative study that Just Ask a Woman helped conduct in 2001 among 800 women aged 25 to 54, 40 percent of the respondents said that they had less than one hour per day for themselves. Yet when asked, "Who has complete control over your typical day?" 38 percent answered "me."[9] Women are the culprits behind their own crazy agendas. When did women decide to become their own worst bosses?

Here is a common response from women on this issue: "I just think taking care of everyone is my job, my role. It's kind of been a tradition for women, that we are the caretakers. I guess it's because we're damn good at it."

Lesson 3. Simplify Your Product or Service to Support Her Life

If you want women's dollars, get in tune with their stressed lives and figure out how to make them easier. It's simple if you are really listening. Make your bank statements understandable. Write the instructions for her cell phone in English. When you show women new ideas or experiment with new programs and services, and their response is, "Maybe this would be good for my sister," it's code for "Why would I waste my few spare minutes on your waste-of-time idea?"

Some women do not have enough time to recharge their cell phones, let alone program some obscure new feature into them. Before you ask her about your new invention, ask her how she spends her day. Find out where you belong. Ask her if she will let you in.

If you are in the service business, talk to your front lines about how they are approaching women. The old adage of smiling and speaking clearly is not enough. You must pay attention to her body language. If she walks up to your counter looking like she is ready for a fight, ease up—don't tense up. A customer service rep once said to me, even before I had gotten my whole complaint out, "I will find a way to make this right for you." I fell in love.

These life-stage portraits of stress tell just part of the story. To link your marketing efforts most effectively to your stressed-out female customers, you must also understand the underlying reasons for her stress. And these feelings are hard to uncover if you are relying on traditional research methodologies. A linear or quantitative line of questioning will not necessarily get you to the "why" of her stress, only the fact of it. That is why I dug deeper, down to the inner world that women feel they deserve.

Women have a rich reservoir of belief about what they deserve. Perhaps no other company has recognized or mined this as well as cosmetics and hair giant L'Oreal. For over 20 years the company has been running a well-known ad campaign tagged with the slogan "Because I'm worth it." The ads and the products are extremely successful around the world because of this simple idea. This approach works because it is true. Underneath their willingness to sacrifice their time and lives for others, women do believe that they are worth it and that they deserve to spend a little more to treat themselves and acknowledge their own value, even if no one else does.

Another example of the value of the worth-it approach was the reaction from women to a creative concept we developed to attract a new generation of shoppers to Saks Fifth Avenue. The tagline, which derived from a strategy of self-worth, was "Live a Little." Female shoppers, especially younger ones who had not frequented this luxury store, smiled and nodded with that "damn right" look in their eyes. To women, "Live a Little" meant, "I deserve to treat myself, and it's about time I rewarded myself for how hard I work." After just a year of running an integrated communications program with this theme, the median age of the Saks shopper dropped by several years.

What Are Women Worth?

Throughout my interviews, I have found very few women who easily assert their worth. Women are comfortable focusing on what their kids need, or how they can reward the people who work with them. But they don't spend much time thinking about what they deserve. I have noticed that the men and women who market to them spend little time thinking about their own needs either. In my role as CEO of Just Ask a Woman, I come into contact with dozens of company CEOs, marketers, publishers, sales leaders, and heads of market research. Sometimes I like to ask them the same questions I ask female consumers.

At the start of a team-building session with a client, I will ask the male and female executives to fill in the blanks, "My name is _____ and I deserve _____." First, there is usually laughter, accompanied by glances and grins and a little embarrassment. Second, the guards go up. As a defense, a couple of the men resort to humor: "I deserve to be somewhere else right now" or "I deserve to be standing in a bar with my best friend." It is usually the women who quietly acknowledge, "I deserve some time off." One woman refused to answer in front of her colleagues and boss but later confided to me, "My husband just went through surgery, and I couldn't let myself say what I was thinking I deserved. I would have lost it." People in companies are no different from consumers. They just hide their stress for other reasons such as job protection and keep up a good company attitude.

Maybe it is just that no one has ever asked women how they

really feel. But understanding a woman's basic sense of self is critical if you are trying to sell to her. You need to ask different questions—and ask them differently to get beneath her reluctance to express her self-worth.

One of the ways I interview women is to invite them to participate in a stylized talk show, instead of the traditional (and in my experience, ineffective) focus group. In this unusual but fun environment, women relax, open up, and answer some very personal questions. In October 2000 I asked 100 women to answer the "I deserve" question. Oddly, it was intended only as an exercise to help them warm up at the beginning of research for a client. Amazingly, unlike many of the marketers I had asked this question, these women decided to tell the truth.

I asked them to fill in the blanks on that same sentence. I have made it a practice in these sessions to answer the tough questions myself first, so that the women don't see me as an unfeeling judge, but as another woman trying to figure things out. (Unfortunately, I have also had to admit when I felt the unhealthiest, how I felt about my period, and why my convertible is compensation for turning 45.) So I started off with my own "I deserve" confession. "My name is Mary Lou, and I quit my job and started this company. I didn't know if it would work, but it did, so I feel I deserve to feel proud of myself." That was the first time I said that out loud. I guess in an age where untested Internet entrepreneurs were making and losing their first millions with so much bravado, it seemed corny to see my admission as a big deal. But for me it was. We are a start-up that actually started up.

The women in the audience smiled back at me: "Yeah, that's good," "You should be proud." Then I turned the microphone over to them.

The first couple of women went straight to the Land of Thanksgiving: "I'm just grateful for everything I have. I don't really deserve anything more." Or "I deserve the wonderful husband and children I have already." These were nice, neat, pat answers. The women answered that way because they wanted to come across as generous, humble, and not self-involved. Women really are caring, but for some of them it is also important to *seem* caring. I did not challenge them at this point because this was their time to say or not say whatever they wanted. If I had jumped on them with a confrontational, "Do you really mean that?" I am sure I would have closed them down to the deeper responses that they would reveal in their own good time. As a marketer, you might observe the way moderators talk to women. The courtroom method of challenging women early on can defeat your efforts to get them to relax and open up.

Tick, Tick, Tick

A few minutes into the session, their "I deserves" took on a new level of reflection and poignancy. Their voices changed from rote to wistful and from tentative to determined.

What do most women feel they deserve, particularly women with families and jobs and responsibilities? The answer is time, time, time. Some women are starved for a weeklong vacation. Others would be grateful for a day. Anything to find time alone.

Here is how some women described their desperate need for time.

One woman said, "I've been working so many hours, and with the kids and all, I really need a vacation, a long one." I asked her how long it had been since she had taken a vacation. She answered, "1986." It was 2001.

Another woman explained, "I am a single mom. I have a 6-year-old who is in soccer and gymnastics, and I work two jobs, so it's a lot to juggle. I feel I deserve a less hectic life, just for one weekend."

Yet another woman said, "I think I deserve a week with not having to be in the car or driving anybody around. I think I deserve a vacation, but what I'd really like is a week around the house by myself. The kids gone, my husband gone, just sitting around, watching old movies and not having to make anybody dinner or take them to volleyball practice and get home at 8:30 at night. I'd like to sit at home and take a bath and watch old movies."

And a woman named Kathryn quietly said, "I deserve one football season off. My husband is a coach. I have two brothers who are coaches, and from July to November, it's just football, football, football."

If you saw Kathryn, you would see a good sport. She was the kind of mom who probably shows up at every game in the team's jersey, drowns in laundry bags full of uniforms, and serves up kegs of Gatorade at the sidelines. She wasn't asking for much. She just wanted some time for Kathryn. As a marketer, can you give women back time as a reward for choosing your product?

A recent radio commercial for UPS described the story of a mom who loves to spend breakfast time talking with her teenage daughter. Then she gets a job as a customer service representative and loses her morning mother-daughter time because she is forced to work more hours because so many customers call to find out if their shipped packages are on track. By hiring UPS, which e-mails customers the tracking information so that they can check on shipments themselves, she gets back what she considers the best reward of all: time.

If you are depending on women to sell your products, your respect for their time can improve productivity. Discovery Toys relies on women to be their customer connection by hosting home parties to sell the toys. Many of the consultants, busy moms themselves, said that the paperwork and the whole process of holding the home parties were taking too much time, instead of letting them focus on demonstrating the toys. At Just Ask a Woman, we

STRESS TEST

What do these insights about women's stress mean to you? Ask yourself these questions:

Your Products

Does your product save her time?

Is it easy to use and understand?

Does it replace something cumbersome or slow that she is using now?

Does it fit with compatible products she may have?

Access

Is it easy to find?

Is it simple to buy?

Does it work without extra parts to buy?

Does it come with a service plan?

Is it easy to assemble or come with simple instructions?

Fitting into Her Life

Does it really work?

Is it safe?

Does it save time versus what she used before?

Does it accomplish more than one task?

Is it fun or smart?

Does is make her happy or relaxed? (Now you're in the winner's circle.)

(*Continued*)

Diagnosis

If your answer to any of these questions is "no," then realize that you are about to walk headfirst into her stress. And she sees you coming. Women resist and reject those things that they can control (you and your products) to make up for the things that they cannot (their kids, their security, their life).

developed a simpler way for women to lead the parties, by reducing a 50-page fine-print training manual into only four index cards of information. When I announced this "Party in a Bag" idea at the company's national convention, 1,200 appreciative moms brought the house down with their applause and approval. Simplifying your interaction with moms is critical.

Lesson 4. Look at Your Product or Service through Her Stressed Eyes

Try this simple exercise. If possible, put your product on your desk. Now, instead of thinking of it as the familiar product you know so well, look at it as if you have just had an insane day with kids and work and traffic and you have a headache and you are really, really stressed-out. What can you read? How small is the typeface? How confusing is it to open? What if you are racing to rip it open to make dinner or to medicate a screaming infant? Does it look like the box is large enough to feed the guests who suddenly drop in uninvited? Does it look like it will break after one washing or use? Remember: her eyes, not yours. The following sections should help you stress-proof your products and services.

Taking Stress to Work

The dual effect of career and home adds another layer of stress to the way women respond to your brand or service. Even as early as the late 1980s, when I was ad director for Avon, I used to get annoyed when media people presented separate media plans for working (vs. nonworking) women. It is hard to find a woman who is not working at something in addition to home and family care, and that pressure is part of nearly every decision she makes. Internally, she does not separate her lives into components.

Working moms face kids who may wish they were home and husbands or partners who may or may not help, and they may or may not have bosses who understand their conflicted feelings. A pregnant woman remarked, "I have three and a half kids, and I just want my employer to realize that I am trying to be good employee, but a good parent, too."

In addition to feeling pulled in several directions, women also feel guilty that they are not working hard enough: "I deserve not to think about work when I'm not at work," declared one woman named Ann. I asked whether she thought about work a lot. "Yes, a lot," she replied. "Right now, tonight, I'm sitting here thinking, maybe I should do this tomorrow, and maybe I should do that. It's just crazy."

This high level of stress at the workplace is resulting in a new phenomenon called *working undertime*. Although both men and women are practitioners of this, women are more likely to feel forced to do it. Women still shoulder 70 percent of traditional household duties in addition to their day jobs.[10] For women, the combination of increasing demands at both home and work stretches the limits of how much they can get done in 24 hours. In addition, with a tight economy, where pay raises are rare and the workloads of those not laid off increase, there is only one way for women to do it all—going underground. This means taking time out of the workday to do errands, research health issues online, and make calls and appointments for the kids. Working undertime is a symptom of trying to do it all while not dropping a ball. How can you tell if your customer is working undertime? How high is your volume of customer calls from females during the lunchtime hours? Do you receive Internet questions about a household appliance from an e-mail address at her office? She is squeezing her many lives into every working minute.

That is why internet sites like Ofoto.com are real boons for women. Instead of ducking out of the office during scarce break times to drop off film for developing, customers can send their digital photos right to Ofoto, which not only develops them but also provides online service for sending pictures to family and friends, who can then also get copies.

In better economic times, some corporations have paid for so-called concierges so that workers could be less distracted by their "consumer chores." Health insurance companies have offered VIP plans (with VIP price tags) that come with your own personal "wife" to deal with claims, referrals, and prescriptions. Johnson & Johnson has onsite dry-cleaning and banking. All these businesses realize that women's consumer lives are intertwined with their professional ones.

Just ask Cathie Black, President of Hearst Magazines . . .

I talked to my friend and client Cathie Black about what she has observed about women's tangled feelings toward work and home. Cathie's lessons come not only from Hearst's millions of readers but also from the women executives who are her clients and her own expe-
(continued)

(Continued)

rience. Cathie pioneered a program for women called "Mind, Body, Soul," for which she gathered over 100 female executives for a three-day session of learning, bonding, and relaxing. She hosted the program for four years and still hears reactions from the attendees: "It was mind-boggling. Women came up to me and wrote me letters afterward. They had not let themselves even free their minds to think about how one-dimensional they had become in their office lives. Women are torn because they want to do a fantastic job at work, but they also want to have a personal life that is valuable, and they want a personal life that is somewhat in balance. Rarely do people, especially men, ask women about their spouses, their children, what is going on in their personal lives. What most women do everyday is kind of check their emotional baggage at the door. Working toward a balanced life isn't something women should apologize for."

This dual home-work stress can actually make women sick. As one woman told me, "I know that stress makes me sick. Stress turns my stomach inside out. When my stomach starts hurting, it's like, 'Okay, I have to go home from work, light a candle, and rest for a while.'" As employers of women and as marketers to them, you probably have felt the costs of stress on your team's productivity.

Working part-time may not be the solution. A study published by the *Harvard Business Review* found that moving from full-time to part-time work actually increases stress. In the article, Karen Messing noted that part-time workers "often inherit the worst schedules. Their services are required during very busy periods. As a result, they don't have any breaks and they work like crazy."[11]

I heard the most touching comments from the women who admitted that they rarely felt acknowledged—not by husbands or kids or bosses: "I have two sons, and I deserve to be loved by them because I've worked hard in giving them their lives. And they never say thank you. Never."

A woman named Maria said, "I deserve more happiness because I work really hard at my marriage, my relationships. I deserve more in return. I deserve recognition for all the little things I do every day that no one helps with, or every one else complains about doing." When I asked her where she would like that recognition to come from, she replied, "My husband. More affection, more recognition, more input into the actual relationship."

Ironically, Maria was one of the women who had earlier recited her "Thanksgiving blessing" where everything was so perfect. It just took a little longer for the truth to come out (reason number 9,000,000 why focus groups in artificial situations do not work).

Some marketers seem to assume that they can just avoid or deny this entire stressful topic. This kind of corporate arrogance was spoofed in the recent movie *What Women Want*. In the movie, Mel Gibson's character, a cocky Madison Avenue creative director, waxes his legs and wears control-top pantyhose to try to understand women's motivations to buy. Like some of his real-world counterparts, however, the character can see women only as cardboard cutouts meant for dating or cooking. In the movie, he does not learn to appreciate the emotions and stresses underlying women's actions until he is hit by lightning. (If only it were that easy.)

Lots of marketers, intentionally or not, skip the stress and go straight to the sell. TV commercials still cook up stress-free living for women. Microwavable meals make it easier for Mom to zip through dinner so that she can hop quicker into the minivan with the kids in the backseat. Then, later at night, coiffed and dressed to the nines, she can go out with her gorgeous, just-turning-gray husband to a sophisticated night on the town in their luxury sedan. That never happens, at least not in a woman's typical day.

She doesn't really want to go anyway. She wants to close the bathroom door and jump in the tub with a gossipy magazine. She wants a nap. She wants to laugh out loud with somebody she is crazy about. She deserves it.

You might be saying, "I know all this." Remember the first statement on the listening checkup? If you are not attracting your fair share of female dollars or retaining women's loyalty, you might also ask yourself, "What am I doing about it?"

Lesson 5. Dial Up the Information and Action; Dial Down the Pressure and Anxiety

The greatest benefits your products, services, and communications can offer are peace of mind, ease, and control. When you are developing new products or advertising to a stressed woman, do not overdo the too-true-to-life portrayals of her stressed life. She may feel like you're rubbing it in. Just get to the solution and let her get on with it. And don't just promise stress-free buying; do something about it. As a woman in Dallas told me, "Enterprise is the only car company my family will rent from because they deliver so you don't have all the hassle of going out to them, standing there to wait, filling out all the paperwork. They come, your car is there, you sign your name, you show your credit card, and you're on your way."

Another woman, who was stressed-out about getting her teenage son's international trip insurance, paid this tribute to Empire Blue Cross/Blue Shield. "I was so prepared for a runaround, but instead this woman said, 'You don't have to call any other department. I can handle it for you over the phone.' I could feel her smiling over the phone. I just kept gushing, 'Thank you, thank you.' I was almost pitiful in my gratitude because someone finally made something easy." It's not just the ads; it's the action.

In each of the remaining chapters you will find the recurring theme of stress. Her stress filter affects the way a woman makes decisions, the way she feels about her self-confidence, the way she reacts to shopping, the way she needs to connect, and the way she wants to run away from it all.

Cracking the Code on Stress

As a marketer, keep these action steps in mind:

1. *Accept her stress; don't compete with it.* Or question it. It's her stress, and it's your job to help her out of it. Think of it as customer relationship therapy.

2. *Pay particular attention to the needs of stressed-out moms.* Moms are the caretakers, gatekeepers, in-home doctors, judges, and psychiatrists. They will shut you out if you are a burden.

3. *Simplify your product or service to support her life.* Just because you like the fancy loyalty program or clever invention you dreamed up does not mean she wants it.

4. *Look at your product or service through her stressed eyes.* You make a nice salary. You have a staff. You have time off (yes, you do; you just aren't taking it). Focus on her reality, not your version of it.

5. *Dial up the information and action; dial down the pressure and anxiety.* Walk the talk. Sympathizing with her stress might make you look nice. Doing something about it makes her happy and makes you money.

In the next chapter you will learn how women make decisions. You can imagine how their stress filters can complicate the process. Chapter 3 will help you navigate the multilayered decision-making processes of women so that they choose your brand.

CHAPTER
3

Deliberate Decision Making

Too many people have railroaded me into things. They were wrong. I'll make up my mind in my own good time.

If Chapter 2's focus has not totally stressed you out, consider how that stress affects the way that women make decisions about your brand. For many women, the pressure they feel from others to *do* is escalated by the pressure they feel from you to *buy*. Chapter 3 is all about how women make decisions—and about how you, as a marketer, can get women to say yes to your brand.

As CEO of Just Ask a Woman and earlier in my career as agency CEO for clients like Procter & Gamble, Avon, and Continental Airlines, I have listened to thousands of women talk about how they make decisions on everything from how they shop to how they diet, invest, dress, and change jobs. No matter what the subject, the conversations have been very personal and complex. Women do not decide lightly.

Anyone who sells or markets to women knows what it is like to wait. The challenge for you as a marketer is to understand why she takes so long to decide and what the key drivers that make her

59

say yes or no are. This chapter decodes the process through a new tool called the *decision quadrant* that breaks out the four components of women's decision making so that you can learn how to get their vote for your brand. First, though, why is she taking so long to decide?

The Waiting Game

After hearing how stressed and pressed for time women are, you would think that they would want to make decisions quickly so that they can get on with their lives. However, the opposite is often true—and particularly frustrating to the marketers in high-stakes businesses such as financial services and the automotive industry, where the wait can feel excruciating to the seller.

A very successful female broker in a financial services company confessed to me, "I hate to say this, but I'd rather work with male clients. They know what they want, they come, they listen, and they do the deal and that's it." She added, "With women, you have to meet with them so many times, going through alternatives, responding to every little thing they read in the paper that day. It's just not as profitable for me." That is a short-term calculation. Women's proclivity for sustaining long relationships (when they are good ones), as well as their longevity and increasing wealth over time, negates that.

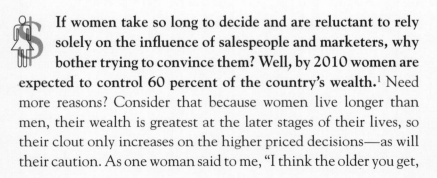 **If women take so long to decide and are reluctant to rely solely on the influence of salespeople and marketers, why bother trying to convince them? Well, by 2010 women are expected to control 60 percent of the country's wealth.**[1] Need more reasons? Consider that because women live longer than men, their wealth is greatest at the later stages of their lives, so their clout only increases on the higher priced decisions—as will their caution. As one woman said to me, "I think the older you get,

the less chances you take with your money." Or another: "My husband takes more gambles. He takes them faster than I would. I would take longer on it." Notice that this woman refers to quick decisions as gambles. Quick decisions equal thoughtless or risky decisions to her.

Women go through a deliberate decision process before they shop. As a marketer, you need to learn which phase she is in. When she is ready to shop, she actually pulls the trigger pretty quickly.

Just ask Miriam Muley, Executive Director of Marketing and Sales at General Motors . . .

Miriam Muley is GM's executive director of marketing and sales for women and diversity, a role enriched by her many years of experience as an agency leader and a marketer for clients like Avon, Clairol, and Spring Mills Industries. Based on research she did in the showroom, she has an eye-opening truth for other marketers who may think that women take a long time to make up their minds: "The conversion rate [from shopping to purchase] in the showroom is generally higher for women than it is for men. When a woman walks into a dealership she is more likely to get a sale closed than a man. She has done her work. She is ready to buy. Also, the African American market, both male and female, has a higher conversion rate than any other female. Don't take them for granted in the selling process." Women's adept use of on-line and offline research prepare them for decision making at the selling moment.

As one woman said to me about the dealer experience, however, "I hate it when a salesman says, 'I can put you in this new car in under two hours. I don't want to be 'put there' that fast.'" Assuming that every browser is a buyer can backfire. Let women let you know when they are ready to buy.

Other industries where women are likely to have done their

homework when they come to your brand include banking and insurance services. Women are unlikely to approach an important high-stakes purchase without doing research on their own. Whether it is ammunition against aggressive salespeople or self-protection, women do a lot of their browsing on their own.

Lesson 1. Know When She Is in Shopping Mode versus Deciding Mode

While impulse and low-risk purchases happen quickly, bigger purchases are backed up by a woman's full decision-making resources. Do not rush her. She will buy when she is ready. Do not be annoyed with her for not buying on the spot. She is not wasting your time; she is testing you to see whether you are worthy of her business. It's about what she is shopping for, but it's also about you. Are you straight with her? Do you treat her questions with respect? Do you look her in the eye or let your eyes drift to the next buyer? Do you interrupt her questions by taking cell phone calls? You are dead if you do. Because she's busy, she's stressed, and she's giving you time she doesn't have.

Before she opens her wallet, she has already gathered and retrieved a lot of information that is important to her.

Four Decisions between Women and Your Brand

When women decide about your brand, an entire underground process kicks in. You must meet the four criteria she uses to decide about your brand. This quadrant can help you decipher how your brand rates with women. As you learn about each quadrant, ask yourself, Is each factor a plus or a minus for my brand? Here is an overview of how the decision quadrant works and how you can apply it to your business.

Quadrant 1: Powerful Memories

In any woman's life, there are products or experiences that have made a huge impact (good or bad) and that color the way she thinks about the brand forever. A brand like the Volkswagen Beetle evoked such a positive powerful memory that the recent resurrection of the model was a smash hit nearly 30 years later. Perhaps you think that the Beetle's cool, retro positioning would attract a new, young buyer. Not so. The new model's average driver is a 45-year-old woman who remembers it from her "first car" days. (I still smile when I recall my own used red 1968 Beetle with an automatic shift that putt-putted me to college and my first job.) Of course, not all powerful memories are positive. Remember the Pinto? Tab? Spam? Women might forgive, but they never forget.

It is important to realize that while powerful memories, good or bad, may not always be top of mind for women, they can be recalled instantly with the marvelous random-access minds that women are so proud of. (I refer to this talent as my garbage brain, filled with millions of long-gone facts that I can retrieve at a moment's notice.) If a brand has a powerful positive memory, it smoothes a woman's decision-making process and paves the way for line extensions that you might introduce. If it is a bad one, you have a hurdle to overcome.

A positive powerful memory can evoke feelings of comfort, reliability, and satisfaction. Personally, I associate some products with indelible emotions, like the thrill of a sharpened cornflower-blue Crayola crayon, the comfort of the red and white Tylenol bottle, and the mother's love in a can of Campbell's Tomato Soup.

Folger's Coffee has one of the most successful long-running campaigns in the category, by associating the aroma of Folgers with "the best part of waking up." The longtime theme music has become an instant wake-up call and memory trigger.

My own powerful memories range from Velveeta cheese, which my Dad grilled into sandwiches, to the first pair of Dr. Scholl's wooden sandals I wore at the Jersey shore. That rectangular block of processed cheese is tied to mental pictures of my Dad putting extra butter on the bread and melting it in a heavy, black frying pan; the sandals, to the smell of sea salt as I walked the boardwalk in Ocean City—I was finally a cool teenager who had abandoned the saddle shoes I wore at my Catholic high school. I cannot look at either product today without the sensation, the emotion, the people, and the feelings attached.

Powerful memories have birthed an emerging business of product bring-backs. Breck shampoo, the elixir for beautiful hair that was popular in the 1960s and 1970s, was reintroduced in June 2002. Remember the hand-illustrated portraits of Breck girls on the back covers of women's magazines? The powerful memory of the fragrance, the golden bottle, and the promise of silken hair should help ease its reentry onto the shelves at drugstore chains.

Powerful memories are not relegated to products. How about an experience like a childhood trip to see the Christmas windows at Saks Fifth Avenue? How about a behavioral memory, like being raised by parents who tucked money each week into individual savings passbooks marked mortgage, school, and vacation? That is how I grew up, so for me the idea of blending my financial assets into a portfolio is as disconcerting as letting mashed potatoes mix with peas on my plate.

Listen to this woman reminisce about Neiman Marcus: "It was the first store I ever shopped in. I had just gotten married. I was 18. They had chairs set up in the vestibule with a newspaper on each one. And they had coffee and tea and blue sugar. It said compliments of the Zodiac Room. So I always think of blue sugar when I think of Neiman Marcus." This woman was nearly 60, yet it was the face of an 18-year-old that smiled through this powerful memory.

Another woman revealed the powerful memories associated with cosmetic powerhouse Clinique: "When I was going to get married, I went to buy makeup. I had a whole makeover done by a woman at the Clinique counter. I said, 'Too bad you can't come on my wedding day,' and she said, 'I can,' and she came and did all my friends and me. So I still use those products years later because she was one of the first people to sit down and say, 'This is what makeup is, and here's what to do with it to make yourself look the way you want to look.'"

Many marketers talk about a brand's DNA. They are actually tapping into powerful memories without even realizing it. The popular concept of *emotional branding* is another example of reaping the value of the feelings that influence brand personality. Imagine the power of mining the emotions that are already in place. Sears is running an advertising campaign that reminds customers that it has always been the place to find what they need for their lives. Chevrolet has introduced favorite songs with references to the brand, like the song "Little Red Corvette" and the line "drove my Chevy to the levee" from "American Pie." It is as much about reminding consumers of a powerful emotional memory as it is about branding the car.

Lesson 2. Try to Understand Where You Fit in Her Life

I have talked to women about nearly every category they buy, and do you know what my first questions are always about? (Hint: It's never the client's product.) I ask, "What's your life like now?" Remember to start off focusing on her life instead of on your brand.

Sometimes my clients get nervous that I am spending too much of our allotted research time on questions that seem personal and peripheral to their business issues. By doing so, however, you will learn more than you ever realized about her motivations, her resistance to buy, and her process for deciding about you. To discover her personal memories, I don't ask, "How do you feel about XYZ?" but, "What's the biggest impact that XYZ had on your life?" Begin with what matters most to her: the life that she and her loved ones live each day. That is where her memories lie.

Powerful Memories, or "No Thanks" for the Memory

For women, powerful memories can work in reverse, too. Remember the chain salon where she got her first bad haircut? Think she will give them another shot? Remember the car driven by the boyfriend who dumped her? Think she is going to buy the new version of that?

Listen to this victim of a bad service experience: "I'd been back 12 times, so I started to keep a list of everything I had been through. I had it nicely delineated in one of the hour and 59 minutes that I sat in the beat-up, nasty old furniture in their waiting room, while I watched Judge Judy all morning." Think she has gotten over that?

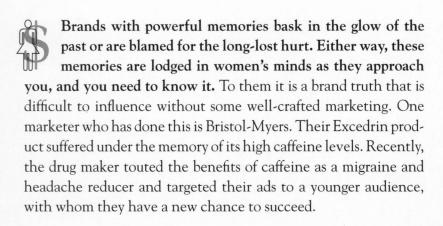 **Brands with powerful memories bask in the glow of the past or are blamed for the long-lost hurt. Either way, these memories are lodged in women's minds as they approach you, and you need to know it.** To them it is a brand truth that is difficult to influence without some well-crafted marketing. One marketer who has done this is Bristol-Myers. Their Excedrin product suffered under the memory of its high caffeine levels. Recently, the drug maker touted the benefits of caffeine as a migraine and headache reducer and targeted their ads to a younger audience, with whom they have a new chance to succeed.

Quadrant 2: Product Legend

Product legend is related to powerful memories, but it often comes from information outside a woman's own experience. Have you ever heard someone describe Nordstrom's? Ask any woman, and you are likely to hear the retailer's service legend as I did: "They don't sell tires, but their service is so great, they'll even take a tire back if you return it." It may be true that many of these women recall an actual Nordstrom's shopping experience during which they enjoyed this extraordinary service. When I probe women on these testimonials, however, many also say, "Well, I've actually never been there, but I've heard about it."

Product legends can be bad news too. How many people still believe that saccharin causes cancer? That Jaguars always break down? That combining Pop Rocks and soda can kill you? Product legend can help you shortcut the decision-making process. Good ones are hard to earn. Bad ones are hard to lose. How is a legend built?

Nordstrom's did it two ways. First was its consistent delivery of customer-centered behavior. Second, and even more critical, the company has done a bang-up job with its public relations activities, as exemplified by the case studies and books written about them, such as *The Nordstrom Way*. By helping to spread the service legend, they are helping women shortcut their decision-making processes when a new Nordstrom's store comes to town. **Women's belief in the legend casts a halo on their actual firsthand encounters because they expect and note great service touches, even if they are not executed at the exact levels that they have heard about.**

I had firsthand experience with another example of product legend when I worked at Avon. Avon's Skin-So-Soft is moisturizing bath oil. For many years, however, the word was out that it was incredibly effective at preventing insect bites. Avon did not want to fan the flames of this legend for two reasons. First, telling women that an indulgent bath product was a good bug killer would kick the heck out of its beauty image. Second, even though the product was resistant toward mosquitoes, it did not have approval from the Environmental Protection Agency or the Food and Drug Administration as bug repellent. So while the press reports and the independent Avon representatives had a field day spreading the legend of the brand (whose sales grew to exceed $100 million), Avon had to stick to the beauty story. Meanwhile, the Skin-So-Soft bath brand started to line-extend in nonbeauty forms such as sprays, sticks, and outdoor candles. The underground success led to top-line results, and the legend became reality when Avon worked to get federal approval to enter the repellent business, which now includes products such as Skin-So-Soft Bug Guard Plus insect repellant spray.

When a brand has a truly golden product legend, such as Johnson & Johnson as a company that is good to moms and babies, even a major crisis can be overcome. For example, even after the tainted Tylenol incident of 1982, when tablets laced with cyanide led to deaths in Chicago, Tylenol was able to regain consumers' trust. By acting instantly to pull the product from the shelves all over the country, even before they knew what was wrong, Johnson & Johnson showed customers that they came first—ahead of profits or the company's own image. Johnson & Johnson waited to restore the brand until the company had invented new tamper-proof bottles. This behavior elevated the phenomenal trust ratings that the brand enjoys to this day—especially among moms who rely on Tylenol for safety.

Can a good product gain a bad product legend? In 2000 Firestone Tires suffered a barrage of lawsuits, bad press, and voracious, competitive assault because of their link to car accidents and deaths. They have since put in higher product standards and have come out with a new ad campaign. No matter what they do, however, my husband and I are reminded of the disastrous incidents all the time. Whenever Joe and I are driving on a highway and we see a burned-out tire shred at the side of the highway, we yell "Firestone!" Not so funny, if you're Firestone. The company continues to work to restore its product's performance and reputation.

Product legends can be created. If your product has good ones, you should leverage them. If they are bad, they can be hard to overcome. If your product is the victim of a bad legend, you need to read about the following quadrants to discover ways to bring women to your brand despite the legend. Getting on a woman's board of directors is a way to start.

Quadrant 3: Her Board of Directors

Before women call the shot on a decision, they rely on their personal board of directors, a cast of trusted advisors that women accumulate throughout their lives. A woman's board of directors is an informal but intricate web of experts drawn from the various segments of her life. For financial decisions, her list could include Uncle Ernie the accountant just as easily as financial commentator Joe Kernen from CNBC. For health care, she looks to her mom and the Internet as well as to her doctor. Understanding her network and the value she places on it can help you earn a seat on her board.

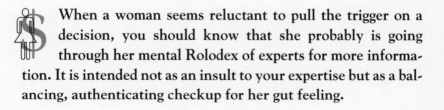 **When a woman seems reluctant to pull the trigger on a decision, you should know that she probably is going through her mental Rolodex of experts for more information. It is intended not as an insult to your expertise but as a balancing, authenticating checkup for her gut feeling.**

Marketers must understand and respect a woman's board of directors and identify how brands can get a place at this table of trust. If you do not know who is on her board, you can find out very easily. Women brag about their boards. They like to tell other women their trade secrets.

Here is a board testimonial from one woman: "I have a cousin that works for Charles Schwab so I have carte blanche to his info. I also live next door to a manager of an investment company, and he's the one I trust with my investments. I trust people that I know. And when I say I know you, I'd mean that I know you well enough to invite you in for lemonade."

For health decisions, a woman's board of directors might include her mother, the nurse down the street, a columnist for a newspaper, or an anonymous friend in a chat room or bulletin board. She also turns to other women, her friends and relatives, who have lived through common circumstances such as having babies and going through menopause. They are an immense source of comfort and advice. As one woman said to me, "I'm lucky because I have seven older sisters and a mother, so anything I run into, between all of them, someone has already gone through it."

ADVICE ON MAKING A DIFFERENCE

"It's interesting because people say all the time, it must have been easier to get to the top of a lipstick company. But that's not actually true, because with the exception of founders, there are no other women. There is still a lot of opportunity. This company was founded on empowering women and giving them independence before they could vote. We were creative about our [woman-focused] vision, but it was still just words on our boardroom walls, not living or breathing, until we simplified it so that everyone from a guy driving his truck with 'the company for women' on it to top executives understood it, so that it could hold the company together."

—*Andrea Jung, chairman and CEO of Avon Products*

Research, both online and off, magazine articles, professional journals, and TV programs are a woman's back-office board sources. In nearly every category I have studied, women have cited their reliance on the Internet for research. For many women, the Internet has evolved into a surrogate friend to be called on for reinforcement or validation.

Lesson 3. Get Women to Talk about You

Many brands find their way onto a woman's hot list through friends' experiences and word-of-mouth endorsement. If she asks a friend what airline she likes, what hotel chain is good for kids, or what SUV she would buy, your company's goal is to be on her board advisor's hot list. Lake Austin Resort and Spa follows up with its customers immediately after a visit in order to fuel their fans with information and referral opportunities. Immediately after a stay, I received a personal note from the spa director, suggestions on exercise techniques from one of the instructors, and a rehearsal routine from a salsa dance teacher I met there. The spa's website and direct-mail programs always include deals for those who return with friends, as well as incentives and reminders to return during each season of the year. I have told dozens of women about this spa, and I keep the resort on my hot list of referrals whenever I am asked.

Assume that membership starts with excellent performance and is then reinforced by strategic viral-marketing efforts among the women who can carry your message better than you can. DailyCandy.com is a trend website that has captured the fickle fashionista audience of New York. Recognizing its appeal as the source of insider information on what is happening in beauty, fashion, and hip night spots, DailyCandy frequently invites members to pass the website on to moms and kids as a way to extend the network of cognoscenti. I have asked and been asked, "Do you get DailyCandy?" more times than I can count.

Lucky magazine is another success story that grew through women's word of mouth and a creative marketing idea. This Conde Nast magazine was designed for women who love to shop, and it has quickly gained a reputation for triggering sales of many of the products that it profiles. The magazine supports women's viral marketing by including stickers that women can apply to the items that they want to find in stores. Any woman who sees another woman with a sticker-covered *Lucky* is practically compelled to ask about it, thereby birthing another customer and reader.

While DailyCandy and *Lucky* did the upfront marketing work, their members and readers do the legwork to grow the franchise.

Just ask Lisa Caputo, President of Citigroup's Women & Co. . . .

In 2000 Lisa Caputo moved from her position as Hillary Clinton's press advisor to a new post at Citigroup. She was brought in to start up a new women's financial services division called Women & Co. Here is her take on the power of a woman's board of directors: "Women choose their financial service provider just like they would choose their doctor. They talk to their friends, and they talk to their family members, and so it is all through word of mouth. I guess you'd call it viral marketing. It's certainly an interesting dynamic, and one that I know instinctively because as a woman, I do it myself." Lisa leverages that word of mouth by treating Women & Co. not just as a lineup of products but as a membership program, with newsletters, master classes, and events. By constantly seeking feedback from female customers, Lisa launched a successful new venture featuring "all the things women want out of a financial institution that will make the system work for her, not just the same financial services wrapped in pink."

Joining the Board

As a marketer, you can wait for women to choose you, or you can put yourself on their short lists. Assuming that your product has talk value, one way to develop your own word-of-mouth campaign is to create a consumer advisory panel of women who are chosen for their relevance to your target audiences' lives, such as moms like themselves. Reward them for testing products with discounts and coupons, and report their reactions in company-wide communications. Be sure to let the panel know how the rest of the group weighed in; feedback is a benefit of participation, too. With a well-executed program, advisors will tell dozens of their friends that they are on your panel, thereby crowning themselves experts on whom friends will call for advice.

You can recruit these advisors whenever you are on the road interviewing women for research. Keep an eye out for those women who not only represent the range of your customer base (age, ethnicity, geography, usage) but also appear to be women who like to be asked their opinions. To keep them motivated, be sure to assign responsibility to a person or department that will not drop the ball but will continually design fresh approaches and supply quick follow-ups. Initiating a panel and then dropping it because of insufficient funding or inadequate staffing sends a bad signal to your best ambassadors. And as good viral marketers, they will tell many more women what you did and did not do. Since women are so busy, consider rotating their terms so that their obligation to the panel is no more than a year, and be sure to give them the choice to opt out and determine the frequency and type of communication that they prefer.

When my associates and I started the Just Ask a Woman Collective, our online research network with hundreds of women, we promised that we would never sell their names or bother them with multiple requests for their opinions. We always keep the questions brief and few so that we do not impose on their time, and every mailing gives them the opportunity to say goodbye to us if they wish.

Athletic shoe companies have lists of road testers who try their shoes and give their feedback to designers. Those people can then be considered experts on shoes that work best, making them in-the-know experts to their families and friends.

Actually, you have many opportunities to develop board members who love your brand. Every time you do market research, you can elect to close the session with a coupon, a feedback form, or an invitation to stay in touch online. Most marketers do not think of research as reciprocal in that way.

Face-to-face consumer research is also a chance to bond with potential brand ambassadors. After the research session ends, moderators typically distribute the honorariums and say goodnight. What a loss. At Just Ask a Woman, we discovered that the women we have interviewed over the years have told so many of their friends about what we discussed. Some even e-mail us to let us know that they have gone to a store or a counter to check out what we showed them. We encourage them to be on the lookout for product introductions or new ad campaigns that their feedback had influenced. If you endorse and validate women's participation in your brand, you will be rewarded with their advocacy and expert status on your behalf.

Quadrant 4: Firsthand Encounters

The fourth variable in a woman's decision process is the one you might suspect would be the first: her actual firsthand encounter with your brand, product, or service.

I remember my first encounter with Target. I went with my

mom, who always brings out the bargain hunter in me. The sheer size of the store brought out the supermarket-sweeps queens in us. We grabbed two giant shopping carts for the after-Christmas sale, and temporarily drunk on the low prices and the abundant merchandise, we had a ball filling the carts. But then I achieved the impossible. I pulled a really cute pink bathing suit off the rack, which was only $14.99 and looked like it would fit even though I did not take time for the hateful dressing-room try-on. That cemented Target as the low-priced but cool, high-style experience for me.

During a woman's first encounter, her senses are really on alert. She notes how your product looks on the shelf, the language and visuals on the package, and the information on the back. This same dynamic works in retail or service companies. For example, if you are in the hotel business, realize that she is watching how your property measures up from the minute she arrives. If she sees or overhears an argument between two front-desk receptionists, their disagreement enters her peripheral memory. She is listening, almost unconsciously, to determine who is right or wrong. She is analyzing whether your employees are helpful, crude, or angry with their supervisors. She is calculating what that will mean to her stay.

Here is another example of a first encounter from the hotel industry, an encounter that resulted in my own personal viral marketing campaign among my traveling friends. About two years ago, my associates and I conducted several Just Ask a Woman sessions in Columbus, Ohio. We checked into a Westin Hotel, which from my memory-legend angle was a comfortable and nice, if not overly luxurious, chain. That judgment changed the minute I got into the room and discovered one of the most fantastic inventions in the history of hotel-room bedding, the Heavenly Bed. As anyone, particularly any woman, knows, there is always that moment of hope when you check into a hotel room. You may pray, "Please be clean. Please have separate shampoo and conditioner. Please don't let there be a psychopath hiding in the shower." (At least, I think these thoughts.) Like any business traveler, I just want to get a decent night's rest at the end of a workday on the road. I could never have expected the nirvana of that bed.

For the uninitiated, the Heavenly Bed is an all-white bed, with lots of extra pillows, a feather pillow mattress, and the kind of high-thread-count cotton sheets I spoil myself with at home. Slipping into a Heavenly Bed erases all the trials of business travel (like narrowly avoiding the Cinnabon stand in the airport or talking your way out of a middle seat on the plane). This firsthand encounter raised the entire Westin brand up to my must-choose brand status. And I have told at least 50 people about this. And counting.

As a marketer, you may be thinking that you can go only so far in controlling a successful firsthand encounter for women. Think again. It is easy to fall into the trap of talking to yourself by assuming that your customers all know you (and love you) as well as you know (and love) yourself. Thinking that she will forgive the little errors. She does not. Each day, new female customers see you for the first time, and they are measuring you on how perfectly you live up to your promise.

A retailer who understands the value of a first encounter is Sephora. Sephora is a one-stop beauty store that houses a broad range of cosmetic brands. The company understood the importance that women place on trying products before buying, especially when the issue is color matching. But they also recognized that women disliked the experience of wrestling with the sometimes overly aggressive counter staff in department stores to get to try the product. At Sephora, all the products are displayed on sleek open shelving to convey department store elegance that is accessible. In addition, the associates circulate silently, wearing just one white glove as a signal of decorum and cleanliness, ready to magically assist customers who want the hands-on application. The first encounter with Sephora makes it easy to leave with a basketful of treats.

Another smartly crafted first encounter is the sampling program developed by the Ortho-McNeil Pharmaceutical, Inc. for their new birth-control patch, Ortho Evra. Because it requires a prescription, the patch might have had no opportunity for a firsthand encounter in the traditional sense. In addition, women's preconceptions about the patch might have led them to think it was large or noticeable or difficult to apply or wear. Ortho created an ad for women's magazines that featured an actual-size, hormone-free patch so that women could see just how sheer, small, and easy to adhere it was—thus creating a firsthand encounter to generate customer interest and response.

Of all the four quadrants, the first encounter is actually the most in your control. The clarity of your brand idea, the advertising and communications that surround it, and even the way it is presented in stores add up to a good first encounter. Marketing *with* women, by inviting their insights into your development process early on, is the way to be sure that you are right from the start.

Are you asking the right questions?

Where did the decision quadrant come from? Actually, we developed it at Just Ask a Woman after asking thousands of women how they decide things. The key was that I asked the right questions, instead of the traditional ones. For example, if you want to know how a woman decides on your brand versus a competitor's, don't just ask why she chooses the other guy. You will get a short, rational answer: "They're cheaper" or "They're closer." Instead, you need to let her deconstruct her decision rationale for you by asking questions that will encourage her to tell you her version of your brand story.

For a retail client, I conducted an exercise in which I pretended I was a woman walking down the street with a competitor's shopping bag over my arm. "What do you know about me, based on this bag?" I asked. The women were able to do an entire data dump on what they believed about that store, their first impressions of it, and how that linked to their current behavior. Powerful memories? "I went there as an 18 year old for my cotillion gown." Product legend? "They have a reputation that models shop there." Board of directors? "My best-dressed friend goes there all the time." Firsthand encounter? "When I went there, I felt like I was cooler than I am." These kinds of answers give you the emotional underpinning of decision making. That feedback highlighted the essence of the brand, the hidden snob appeal, the exclusivity, the "not-for-me-but-I-want-it-to-be" insight.

By asking the right questions, you can learn how a woman rates you in her personal decision quadrant. However, there is one more barrier between her and your brand, and that is the decision deal breaker: the relationship she has with the seller of your product.

Let us begin with the higher-end product and service categories. Typically, the selling process starts in a very linear way—the way that companies think, What are your financial goals? What kind of policy are you looking for? What kind of house do you need? Net: What is the point?

That is not necessarily what a woman thinks when she shops. She wants to see if, like her, you ask, "What's the bigger picture here?" She wants to understand what you stand for and whether you or your brand fit with her needs.

Listen to this woman: "I want to understand before I take the plunge. I had a conversation with a broker. All he wanted to know was how much money I had to invest, which I divulged, and then he says, 'Well you can do this, and I can do that.' And I said to myself, 'I didn't say I want you to do it. I want to know first what I want to do.' They don't have the time to explain it to a woman, because they think that you don't understand the financial concepts or it's just too much for you to process at one time."

Start with a little history. Financial advisors might try asking, "Tell me about some of the better or worse experiences you have had with financial companies before. Can you share a little bit about your financial situation growing up?" In real estate, slow it down: "Why are you looking for something new? Where were you before? What made you happiest about where you lived before? What would you like to change about your lifestyle?"

Get ready to learn more than you might have wanted to, but also prepare to understand why she wants it, not just what you are selling. Is she worried about losing money again? Did she fire her last advisor because of results or because of bad communication? Did the sales representative provide sufficient follow-up? Does she really want a smaller home, or just one that doesn't remind her of a bad marriage? Women make decisions in the context of their histories, their experiences, and the effect the decision might have on important people in their lives. It is about the result, but also about so much more.

By listening to her story, you will learn whether she has had a powerful memory, whether she believes your product legend, whether you are on her board of directors' endorsed list, or whether she is happy or skeptical based on her own experience. The conversation itself will be the beginning of a trusting relationship, and the relationship with her is critical—over and above the decision quadrant—because it is the make-or-break factor for your brand.

It's Not Business; It's Personal

Think of your own experiences when you were trying to close a deal. In my years in the ad agency business, I suffered through the interminable process of new account reviews. Just when we thought we had made our case with great ideas to win a new account, the waiting game ("We'll get back to you") would begin. First, the silence. Next, the cryptic phone call about a specific copy line in the pitch. Then, the comparative comments: "Why did you decide to do X when we've heard (from another competing agency, of course) that Y is the way to go?" Our frustration would grow to annoyance to desperation—and then depression until the final call.

While the men on the agency team would focus on the creative work ("How could they not love this idea?"), I would focus on the relationship. I would wonder, "Is it something I said or did during the pitch that confused them?" and "Did they connect better with the other agency CEO than with me?"

Sometimes, we won. When we were a close second, the client chose another agency for just what I projected: a belief in the people, rather than the creative idea. I found that particularly true when female clients were the deciders. You know that expression, "It's just business; it's not personal?" That is baloney, especially when women are the decision makers.

So why, when companies sell to women, do they forget that? So often I have heard my male colleagues tell a prospective client, "Here's what we can do better than agency X." I always found the more eye-opening approach was to ask, "What was it about your former agency relationship that you liked, and what would you never want to repeat?" Recognizing the personal reasons behind the facts helps you craft the right sales appeal to women.

It Is a Matter of Trust

From your point of view, your interaction with female consumers may be a transaction. To your female customer, it is as much about how she feels about your brand or service personality and attitude as it is about the facts.

Ask a broker what it is like to advise a woman on her finances. "She takes too long to decide." "She doesn't have as much money as a man." "She's not that informed about her money." "It's too much work." The broker is thinking about the end goal of the transaction.

Ask a woman what it is like to get advice from a broker. "He's barely out of school, and it wasn't even a good school." "I've rejected better ideas than the ones she's proposing." "I've been burned before but never again!" She is thinking about the quality of the relationship, her own confidence, and her personal history.

An ad campaign for J.P. Morgan Chase proclaims, "The right relationship is everything." Rather than emphasize the product sell, the advertising uses a tongue-in-cheek style to show how the bank cares about relationships. In one spot, a couple stands outside a Chase branch, and the woman is so enamored with the bank's services that she is convinced that the ATM slot makes a sound like a kiss.

This trust-based tug-of-war is not limited to the financial services industry. Hairdressers complain that their clients "don't really know what they want when they sit in my chair. . . . I have to tell them." Doctors bemoan the effect of direct-to-consumer advertising and online medical journals: "She's asking all these questions about things she doesn't understand. I don't have time to explain."

To feel certain, women ask a lot of questions and do a lot of listening before they can form a trusting relationship. Some of the questions are not even meant to get at a woman's needs. She has other people in her life who depend on her decisions, and she takes everyone else's needs into account, too. Will the kids be comfortable on this sofa? Will my husband enjoy this vacation? Could I bring this to the potluck party and not look cheap?

Lesson 4. Add Some Love to Your Marketing Mix

Let's face it: Many new product entries are derivative of existing ones, and many new products fail each year. Can you find a way to add a relationship element to your product to connect with women's lives and build trust? For example, a new ad campaign for Dawn dishwashing detergent tells the story of Dawn's grease-cutting benefit on saving ducks that are covered in grease from industrial spills. Gentle to ducks, helping the environment—makes you feel good just to wash pots. If your product or service is one of many competitive entries, as many are, then you better add something to the relationship to make you talk-worthy.

In New York City, there is an exclusive spa called Bliss that has gained a great reputation for treatments, even in a city where there are more than enough terrific day spas. Bliss works at it. One woman I interviewed commented after her visit, "The masseuse personally sent me a thank you note, saying 'I hope you enjoyed your experience.'" That kind of behavior transformed a first encounter with a potentially intimidating spa visit into a familiar relationship—and the woman is still talking about it.

Banana Republic strengthens bonds with its frequent credit card customers with a LUXE card, which features an exclusive upgrade on services such as free shipping for items bought online and free in-store alterations (which is rare for women, especially at this price point). In addition, frequent discounts and private sales keep her coming back. And yes, talking.

Now, you may think that this over-the-top performance applies only to luxury brands. Not true. Why does Starbucks feature cozy seating areas in its take-out coffee shops? Why does Wal-Mart have greeters? They are attending to the importance of a creating an atmosphere of conversation, of a kind of retail friendship.

The Who behind the What

Women's final gut-checks come from their relationships with the human beings connected to your brand or service. Your salespeople, brokers, receptionists, customer service reps, and retailers can seal or wreck the deal.

A good relationship allows women to give you the opportunity to perform. A bad one sabotages your chances. While this may be true with both male and female customers, I have observed that men are more tolerant of weak customer representatives while women become more wrapped up in their actions and personalities. As one woman said to me, "It's the chemistry. You meet; you get together. You're making a marriage here. And if you don't have a trust, and the chemistry doesn't work, then move on."

One of my insurance-company clients acknowledged that while the tedious process and frequent runaround of the claims approval process are considered a negative by both men and women, this behavior of personnel in telephone claims annoys women more. And when women are annoyed, the trust factor declines, the anxiety increases, and their usage of your customer service's 800 number escalates. That lack of love costs you money.

Just ask Bonnie Reitz, Senior Vice President for Sales and Marketing at Continental Airlines . . .

Bonnie Reitz is senior vice president for sales and marketing for this turnaround airline, and her recognition of women's unique service and relationship needs is one of the keys to her success: "Female business

(continued)

(Continued)

travelers are very precise and disciplined in their planning. They follow the rules more, so they get a little more agitated when somebody gets out of line and butts in front of them, and are not tolerant of us if we let anyone butt in front of them. We are more of a customer service business than most. Our life is people. The more we know, the better we can serve them. Let them train us in what it is they want from us, and then let us give that to them, so that they are recognized as the important travelers they are." In other words, Bonnie suggests that customers can actually train your people in how to get their business. With women, it is not a matter of selling. It is about understanding their needs.

Stop Selling and Start Listening

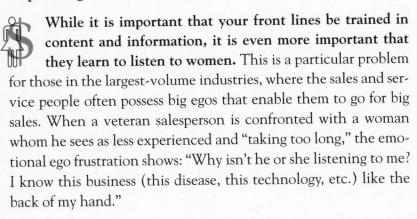**While it is important that your front lines be trained in content and information, it is even more important that they learn to listen to women.** This is a particular problem for those in the largest-volume industries, where the sales and service people often possess big egos that enable them to go for big sales. When a veteran salesperson is confronted with a woman whom he sees as less experienced and "taking too long," the emotional ego frustration shows: "Why isn't he or she listening to me? I know this business (this disease, this technology, etc.) like the back of my hand."

If you are a man, you may be recalling hundreds of conversations with the women in your life, such as your late arrival at an event due to a woman's wondering, "Should I wear this or that?" You may remember restaurant arguments springing from delayed ordering: "Well, should I have the salad? I really want the sandwich, but that might be too heavy. Besides, the waiter said the special is really good." If you are a female, you may be protesting,

"That's not me; I'm a quick decider." Well, if you say so. However, you might also see yourself in this process occasionally, but you attribute it to being wise and not to waffling. (I personally attribute it to being a Libra.)

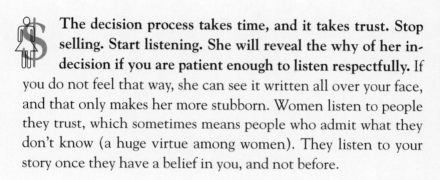 **The decision process takes time, and it takes trust. Stop selling. Start listening. She will reveal the why of her indecision if you are patient enough to listen respectfully.** If you do not feel that way, she can see it written all over your face, and that only makes her more stubborn. Women listen to people they trust, which sometimes means people who admit what they don't know (a huge virtue among women). They listen to your story once they have a belief in you, and not before.

Lesson 5. Get on Her Side before You Get on Her List

She does not know you or your brand or your intentions. She does know and trust the people in her life who care about her. When a car dealer tries to ingratiate himself to a woman by putting down the dealership down the street (when she mentioned that she likes the way their mechanics treat her), he is hurting himself and looks like a sore loser. Do not disrespect her sources or experts. Women will let you in when they trust you, and that trust does not come easily, as the next story proves.

Trust First, Money Second

Building a solid, trusting relationship with female customers is the key to developing loyal, long-term relationships. It is not just *what* you sell, but the *how* and the *who*.

I heard an interesting story from a high-equity broker at a major investment house who revealed the gap between the way men look at a sale as a transaction and women look at it as a relationship: "There was a potential customer, a widow who had inherited $20 million when her husband died. She was shopping the various investment banks to find the right firm to invest and manage her money. My boss thought it would be a good idea to team me up with a female associate so that the customer would feel comfortable. My associate, Sandy, was pregnant at the time, and she and this female prospect really hit it off during the early qualifying interviews. Like our competitors, we worked up a plan for how we would handle her money. I knew our plan was the best in every way for this customer.

"When it came time to decide, she chose us, with a big 'but.' Sandy was on maternity leave, and we had brought on another female advisor who would manage the account with me in Sandy's absence. Despite the fact that this prospect would lose significant dollars every day she delayed the go-ahead on our plan, she insisted on waiting until Sandy came back. I thought that was crazy. How could she give up this great deal?"

This young broker was astounded when I said, "Maybe she really liked Sandy and wanted her to benefit from the transaction. With that kind of wealth, a month here or there probably isn't a big deal to her. Her trust in Sandy was." He was still incredulous. He was focusing on the transaction. She was interested in the relationship as well.

This preference for relationship works at the low cost–high emotional levels, too: "I've gone to this hair salon for five years. I love the woman who cuts my hair, and when she left for a seven-month sabbatical, I didn't go back. I like the salon, but I followed her."

Personally, I have been loyal to the Minardi hair salon in New York City even though its Upper East Side location has never been convenient for me. My trust in the stylists' talents has kept me as a customer for 10 years.

Women are powerful, deliberate decision makers. How can you earn their trust and overcome this decision-making process so that her final decision favors you?

Cracking the Code on Decision Making

1. *Know when she is in shopping mode versus deciding mode.* Find out what outcome she is looking for today. If she says, "I'm ready to buy a car," she really is. Get the paperwork ready now. If she says she is just looking, that means she is just looking. She is filling her mental shopping list with ideas, prices, and comparisons. What is important is that your front lines listen and understand where the woman is in her readiness-to-buy cycle.

2. *Try to understand where you fit in her life.* So much new product research is about how to make a better widget. All that invention is about is you. What about her? If you back up your investigation into why, where, and how she uses you, you will be able to train your front lines in what matters—not just what you think sells. An added financial benefit is that you may end up streamlining your portfolio to achieve more efficiency for both of you.

3. *Get women to talk about you.* Use your current customers as your source of information and reference on your future ones. It is not just about the sample or the survey. Give her an extra sample or gift certificate to give to her friend. Ask your loyal customer to pass the word in exchange for some reward. If you bring your customers in for research, never let them leave without a gift (coupon, trial-size sample, etc.). At the end of our sessions at Just Ask a Woman, many women are ready to be disciples for the brand. Why not give them the tools to spread the word?

4. *Add some love to your marketing mix.* Women have so many alternative products and services from which to choose. Give them a reason to choose you. Women know that brands adopt various causes to show their good citizenship and to create a do-gooder halo. They expect it, and when the fit is right, they respond. However, that does not let you off the hook from humanizing your brand with her. Can you build some value into your information website that answers what is on her mind? Can your customer services people learn to speak woman?

5. *Get on her side before you get on her list.* When a woman makes decisions based on her board, you are the one in the shaky seat. This is not about overturning her existing choice. It is about her choosing you. Imagine that you run the sales force of a pharmaceuticals company. Here is a lesson you can share with medical offices. If a female patient says, "My sister is a nurse practitioner, and she said there's a problem with this drug," don't say, "She's wrong." Acknowledge that there are questions about the drug but that in your experiences with other patients you have seen a lot of satisfaction and results. Women listen to contrasting opinions; they don't listen to put-down opinions.

What happens when this decision process hits the retail store? The next chapter introduces you to the vigilante shopper, a woman who is not necessarily buying what you are selling.

CHAPTER

4

The Vigilante
Shopper

I'm a you've-got-one-chance-to-screw-up shopper,
and that goes for everything I buy.

W hen they are not stressed, some women actually like to
shop. In other words, when they are on vacation, when
money is no object, and when time is not a factor, women
like to shop. (I think that adds up to about two weeks in a typical
woman's life span.) In the real world, a woman's stress filter and
her needs for service can make shopping a chore, not a leisurely
pastime. In the last chapter I introduced you to the deliberate way
she approaches her purchasing decisions. What happens when
these realities come face to face with the world of retail? Women
morph from reasonable human beings into vigilante shoppers.
They approach the shopping experience with a take-no-prisoners
attitude that demands that they will get what they pay for. In this
chapter you will meet the vigilante shopper, learn how she affects
your success at the cash register, and discover why she demands
your attention.

Despite their own busy, working lives, women are still responsible for buying most of what is needed to make their homes and families function. Food, clothing, appliances, automobiles, furnishings, computers, you name it: Women are calling the shots. With limited time and money, women have learned the retail ropes the hard way, and they are rebellious and impatient with an industry that has neglected their needs for service, efficiency, and value.

I have spoken about the frustration that female shoppers cause many major corporations, and I have been interviewed as an expert on the topic by national media. My authority comes from having spoken to hundreds of women who shop drugstores, mass merchandisers, department stores, luxury boutiques, car dealerships, and stores dedicated to home, beauty, and personal care.

When I see that bumper sticker, "When the going gets tough, the tough go shopping," I know it is true. I have to stop and think what happens when a brand confronts a tough shopper. Given the extraordinary stress in women's lives, as cited in Chapter 2, today's female shoppers are tough. With Chapter 3's backdrop of their deliberate decision-making process, women are determined to get their way with retailers. This means that they may take their anger out on you, the marketer who is trying to sell to them.

Despite warnings about the power of female consumers, the retail sector seems to ignore this advice. Consequently, many companies have suffered huge sales declines during the past several years. Quarterly results from retailers including department stores like Sears and Macy's and apparel chains like the Gap and Banana Republic, as well as many national outlets for housewares, beauty, and computers, have been stagnant or declining over the past two years. Only a few retailers, such as Wal-Mart, Target, and Kohl's at the low end and some of the smart specialty retail marketers such as Coach and The Limited at the other end, have shown growth indicating that they seem to be listening to women and taking action.[1]

For that reason I decided to adopt the confrontational language of vigilante shoppers in this chapter. I feel that I need to acknowledge up front that it is not my inclination to talk in militaristic metaphors. As a woman in business, I have always felt alienated when my male colleagues persisted in using military examples at the office, especially those men whose wartime experience came from watching reruns of M.A.S.H. (The ones who actually served can get away with it.) Ever hear someone in a meeting say, "So, are we locked and loaded?" or "We're gonna take the hill." Or how about, "We're going to take them out" (a kind of Al Capone twist). What's next? Brands that go AWOL?

However, I stepped over to the dark side for this chapter because I think it is the only way to break through any lingering misperceptions about female shoppers. Perhaps the use of the aggressive imagery of vigilantism will shake up retailers' lethargy. **Vigilante captures the attitude of today's female shopper, who is tired of waiting for retailers to respect her needs. She sometimes feels angry and ignored, so now she is taking customer service into her own hands. She is on a mission to get satisfaction, and you are in her sights.**

Whether you are a retailer or a manufacturer who depends on retail partners, this chapter exposes the landmines of retail so that you can see where your retail channel succeeds or fails with women.

She Is on the Hunt

Women's retail landmines comprise three territories:

- *Border surveillance*. This phrase captures her preset perceptions of the store's image and environment, as well as her first impressions when she enters the store. This moment is critical to retailers because she will continue out the revolving door if she sees something that bothers her. An example of this is the layout of some Banana Republic stores where the checkout line is right next to the entrance and the women's floor is upstairs, out of reconnaissance view. I have seen women notice the long, snaking checkout line and decide to abandon their visit because of the vibes of stress in advance.

- *Patrolling the selling floor.* This is her in-store inspection, where she walks the tightrope between dodging aggressive salespeople and searching for one when she finally needs one. As a marketer, you may hope that she is checking out your merchandise. Instead, her time crunch is driving her to worry about checking out, period.

- *Nailing the mission.* Ironically, when she is ready to give you her money, you are nowhere in sight. All your good merchandising efforts are left in a heap if she weighs the cost of buying against the cost of aggravation.

In each of these areas there is an opportunity for retail to reform itself for women. Each landmine will reveal usable and simple lessons in customer service so that you can create buying experiences that women will love and prefer. Linked to each will be ways that you can anticipate a woman's retail radar and become her ally, instead of her target (three military hits in one sentence!).

This is an appropriate moment to admit the real reason for this somewhat heavy-handed approach. As I said in the introduction to this book, women are buying or influencing the purchase of 85 percent of what is sold in this country.[2] Eighty-five percent of your volume is something you cannot ignore. If you are not getting your retail platform right for women, you are not getting your fair share of their dollars. To make improvements, you must see and hear what is happening in stores from a woman's perspective.

Retailers in Denial

You would think that the dominance of women in retail is old news for retailers, but it isn't. For the past two years I have been invited to speak at the annual meeting of the Retail Advertising and Marketing Association, the trade association with members from leading retailers from mass to prestige. At each talk I received a lot of laughs (and high ratings) from the audience simply by sharing the truths of what women think about them.

Association president Tom Holliday acknowledges, "The smart retailers 'get' women. They know that women will be sitting when the music stops. But there are a lot of stores, so many being run by men, that don't really have the appreciation that they should for women. I think they are more aware of women, but that's not to say that they are doing more about it. Women own their brands, and they better make them happy."

Making women happy starts with taking them seriously. For many years, however, the image of female shoppers was pretty funny. The joke was that when women shopped, they were out of control. Just remember *I Love Lucy*, with Lucy and Ethel dragging home huge shopping bags to hide from Ricky and Fred, who, of course, would shake their knowing, indulging heads.

As a little girl, I remember watching cartoon gal pals Wilma Flintstone and Betty Rubble scream, "Charge it!" and scramble for rock-bottom bargains in a prehistoric bargain basement. Even today, it is easy to get a smile out of women's penchant for buying shoes (which truly are one of life's shopping pleasures since, unlike new clothes, they fit and look great even if you've put on a few pounds).

Unfortunately, the cliché of women as ravenous hobby shoppers is dying a too-slow death. Just read the news accounts of the many retailers who, year after year, seem surprised when their inventory does not sail out the door at the holidays. Why do they always blame the weather instead of their own behavior? It is time for retailers to get acquainted with their worst nightmare: the vigilante female shopper. She is not pitted against other women in a buying fever (well, she might be if it's the bridal gown sale at Filene's Basement or the white sale at Bloomie's). The object of her anger is you, and as the stress in her life increases, her intolerance for shoddy customer service increases, too.

She's Mad as Hell and She's Not Going to Take It Anymore

Actually, women have been complaining about the retail experience for a long time. However, over the past three years of interviewing female consumers for retailers like Saks Fifth Avenue and Toys R Us and for brands that depend on retail partners, such as General Motors, Estee Lauder, Motrin, and Kellogg's Special K, I have observed a significant change. Women have shifted their frustration into retaliation. They are no longer putting up with the anxieties and annoyances of the retail scene. They are walking out, talking back, and devising techniques to get satisfaction despite "the system."

Remember the quote at the beginning of this chapter? That same vigilante shopper continued, "If I have a complaint, and they start that 'I have to go and talk to the manager' game, I'm out the door, and I do not come back. And when they screw up, I make sure they know it immediately."

This chapter introduces you to lots of other outspoken consumers in an effort to clear up any vestigial perceptions of female shoppers. In addition, I share advice and examples from retailers who are doing it right.

Landmine 1. Border Surveillance

The first landmine is border surveillance. Women tell me that this reconnaissance starts even before a woman steps into a store.

Based on past experience, she has a premonition about the store atmosphere before she pulls into the parking lot. If it is a discount store, she is armed for the chaos, the disarray, and the slow checkout. If it is a midlevel department store, she grits her teeth in anticipation of the inconvenient layouts of the floors, the lack of restrooms, and the scarce sales help. In luxury emporiums, she steels herself for the icy stare of the sales associates unless she is dressed to kill in a suit of armor from the Gucci brigade.

Let us contrast this to the way a man walks into a store. Based on checking out this theory many times with both genders, I propose that women and men shop differently. In an article he wrote for the *New York Sun*, Russ Smith described how he shops: "I don't browse or chitchat with salesmen at stores. It's a quick trip to Paul Stuart, choosing a suit or slacks quickly, then slapping down a credit card and getting on with the day." Not so fast, women would say. As women walk through the door of your store, they observe everything about the store environment (unlike a man, who is likely to head straight for the shirt department if he wants to buy a shirt). With women, all senses are on alert. Is the lighting glaring or dark? Does the air smell good? Is the first floor noisy? Is it clean and neat, or, as one woman said, "Is there crap lying all over the place?"

Border surveillance is not just my theory. Anthropologists and psychologists have studied it, including anthropologist Helen Fisher, who examined this uniquely female skill for noticing details in her book *The First Sex*. She wrote that while "men are good at compartmentalizing their attention . . . women more regularly think contextually, they take a more 'holistic' view of the issue at hand. That is, they integrate more details of the world around them, details ranging from the nuances of body posture to the position of objects in a room."[3]

This ability to notice and remember and then connect those memories to emotions was the subject of a study published in the *Proceedings of the National Academy of Sciences* in July 2002. This study, which tested a series of photos shown to men and women, affirmed that women's brains are better organized to perceive and remember emotions. Turhan Canli, an assistant professor of psychology at State University of New York–Stony Brook and a leader of the study, said, "A larger percentage of the emotional stimuli used in the experiment were remembered by women than by men."[4]

Consider the many emotional scenes that retail presents. Women eavesdrop on the lecture by a haughty sales clerk who refuses to take a return from a customer who lost her receipt. Women observe the piled-up, cast-off bathing suits in a dressing room while disinterested clerks gossip outside the fitting room. Women cringe at the sound of horns blaring in the lot while a young woman with babies slowly steers her overloaded stroller from the store. **Women notice not only the events that affect them directly, but also the ones that contribute to the overall retail environment. As a mar-** **keter or a retailer, you must assume that she doesn't miss a trick. Unless you are paying as close attention as she is, you are not seeing your store through her eyes.**

Just ask Dan Brestle, President of Estee Lauder . . .

As the president of one of the largest beauty companies in the world, Dan Brestle has spent a lot of time in his 24 years there learning about women. He tells this real-world story from an internal meeting about how much women notice people, especially other women: "Women are so aware of the attire and surroundings of other women, it never ceases to amaze me. Here's a funny story. I had a staff meeting with about 15 people. I am the only guy in the room. This was one of those boring staff meetings that we talked about whether it was okay to make closing time on Friday at four o'clock and casual this and that. One of my

(Continued)

senior people, Eunice, walks in about 10 minutes late. I can see by this time, all their eyes are rolling, they are so bored to death. So, I stopped the meeting and I say, 'Has anyone heard what I'm saying?' And they said, yeah, OK, and then I say, 'What are the color of Eunice's shoes?' Not one person missed it. They knew from her shoes to her hair what she was wearing. With that one glance when she walked in, they knew how she was put together. Guys do not do that."

That kind of awareness of details shows why successful cosmetic marketers like Dan put so much time into what might seem frivolous—the sleek packaging, the skin feel of the makeup brush, the stamping of a logo onto the surface of a pressed powder product. It is more than a detail. It can seal the deal.

With that perspective on how women observe details, close your eyes and picture the entrance to your store, the counters, the salespeople, and the buzz. Better yet, open your eyes and walk around with the observational powers of a woman. Is there clutter that you have been ignoring? Sound systems that grate? Associates' eyes averted from the customer? Is the merchandise set so low that little kids can grab it? These are what she sees—and what she remembers.

Lesson 1. Make a Good First Impression; She Is Watching

As a retailer, you have lots of costs to manage, and you may think that you cannot add staff to welcome shoppers, clean up left-behind inventory, or walk the perimeters of the store. But what about the people who are placed at the counters nearest the entrances? Are they trained to look up and into the eyes of women as they walk in or walk by? Can they be rewarded for extra steps that keep the entrances clear, clean, and inviting? Could they be trained in knowing the basic layout of the store since they are the ones who are likely to be asked where everything is?

Back to that first retail encounter, does anyone look up and greet her? This is a lesson that Wal-Mart and Old Navy learned years ago. They place greeters at the door to welcome shoppers and make a personal connection. The Old Navy greeter raps the greeting, which is completely consistent with the brand's fun factor. Recently, I observed the same practice in upscale retailers such as Tiffany. They recognize that one of the luxuries women seek is the sense of being recognized and welcomed before they even spend a dime.

Just ask Paul Higham, Former Chief Marketing Officer of Wal-Mart . . .

Wal-Mart has grown to be the largest company in the world by pleasing customers, most of whom are women. Paul Higham described to me the importance of validation: "You and I and virtually everybody in the world have gone into a store where the attitude or behavior or visual cues make you wonder whether or not you are wanted in that location. I have always felt that as a retail practitioner you have an obligation to create an environment where nobody has any doubt as to whether they are wanted. That is part of belonging. We desperately as human beings want to be accepted and to belong. The most natural tendency for human beings is not to make eye contact, to want to turn away and not get involved. But it is diametrically opposed to what gives comfort to human beings, and that is to be acknowledged."

 The ubiquitous Wal-Mart greeter is not just about being nice. It is about reminding customers that they are truly welcome there. Women understand this silent language because in their own lives they are often the ones to create welcoming homes and to help visitors feel at ease. Of course, the greeting can be a vulnerability, too. While women want to be acknowledged, they are not looking for an extended conversation or a sales pitch. (Witness most women's reaction to "May I help you?": "No thanks; just looking.") How many diners shrink from the too-familiar, "Hi, I'm Heather, and I'll be your server tonight." (On the restaurant front, the unspoken relationship killer can be the overly fragranced waitperson. Ever received your pasta in a cloud of L'Air du Temps?)

If anything, the best secondary role for a greeter is to be a rapid in-store locator or information source. If a woman asks, "Where's the lingerie department?" or "Where's the restroom?" and the first person she meets hesitates or gives the wrong directions, she is already putting negative checks on your brand. The friendly but clueless greeter can backfire.

The hotel industry has begun to recognize the importance of that first relationship at check-in. Ritz Carlton hotels are famous for keeping customer data up to date: When your car or taxi pulls up to the curb, the bellman will let the front desk personnel know that you are coming so that they greet you by name or even say, "Welcome back to the Ritz Carlton, Mrs. Quinlan." That is a great feeling when you have just come from a long flight. Wyndham Hotel's By Request Program retains information on all its former guests so that each room is stocked, located, or prepared in the way that the guest prefers. Prefer a room near the elevator? No problem. Perrier in the minibar? As you wish. Return guests walk in with anticipation of a positive experience, rather than dreading what will happen.

Ever walk into a room that is not ready? I had thought I was upset on a recent business trip when I went into my hotel room and noticed that there was an empty water bottle on the desk and that the chairs were askew. That paled in comparison to my reaction when I stepped into the bathroom and discovered an unflushed toilet and a raised seat. Still dirty or still occupied? This kind of negligence is particularly upsetting to women who feel vulnerable on the road (not to mention that women internalize the idea that "my own house is cleaner than this, and I don't have daily maid service"). Leaders in service businesses cannot underestimate the white-glove expectations of female business travelers. Their heads of housekeeping ought to be considered the chiefs of customer service because that is one of the key concerns of female road warriors.

Adequate training is certainly an ongoing challenge in the retail and services industries, especially with high turnover and questionable skills ("Fries with that?"), but women are not interested in the backroom issues facing retailers. They want to know what you are doing to earn their dollars. One woman made a comparison to Disney: "If you go to Disney World, go to the guy who sweeps up the street after the parade. If you ask him where such and such a ride is, he can give you the fastest directions because they all have to be trained in it first. There is no reason why people in the stores shouldn't have the same training."

Bad border behavior is not limited to traditional retail stores. Women in surveillance mode encounter it when they enter the auto dealership, the broker's office, and even an Internet retail site.

ADVICE ON TRAINING

"Serving women's needs is a little easier for us because when you take a look at our work force, it's 75 percent women. So, the emotional connection to understanding the needs of women is terribly well served by this organization. You see it in our sales associates who undergo tremendous training in terms of understanding needs and styles at the consumer level. You will see it in our marketing, which talks about how the female consumer is quite diversified. And the other way we speak to women is through our charitable endeavors, where everything we do is aimed at women's health issues, such as Fashion Targets Breast Cancer and Women in Need."
—*Christina Johnson, CEO of Saks Fifth Avenue*

She Sees You Coming

Consider one of women's most dreaded shopping missions: the auto dealership. There, she is at her most vigilant because the expense risk is high and she cannot afford to make a mistake. She has done her homework, and she knows the drill like the back of her hand.

As she opens the glass door to the showroom, her eyes are wide open: "I walked into a dealership, and they have the whole system of which sales guy is up next, and I don't necessarily want who's next. The sales guys were all standing in a line, and I thought, 'Well, he looks friendly; I'll talk to him.' But they wouldn't let me. I thought, 'Why don't I get to choose who I deal with?'" Women are aware that the dealership rotates its salesmen either to spread the commissions around or to match their salesperson to her. A woman will find a way to avoid the person on deck so that she can work with someone she perceives as acceptable. Conversely, those dealers who know when to back off and when to approach get huge accolades from the women they serve.

By now, you know that women look closely at you for clues to your performance. But did you know that they also believe that you are looking at them and making judgments about who they are and what they want?

A woman told me this story about buying a car: "Sometimes I actually feel like I have been ignored. It's like they're thinking, Shouldn't you be over in the used car sale lot? I feel that way. Like I'm not being treated seriously. They just want to know where my husband is."

Describing the once-over she got in a bank, one woman said, "When you go into a financial services institution and they're treating you differently, you notice it immediately. The bank vice president or president doesn't come out to greet you, because if you're wearing clothes that look like you just took your kids to school, you don't look like anyone to them. As opposed to your husband that day, who's wearing a suit because he's headed to work."

Stores that do not judge will win: "I like that store because the sales help comes to you. You don't have to find them. No matter how I'm dressed, dressy or down, they treat you with respect. Some other stores, if you're not dressed up, they kind of stay away from you. You feel like security could start trailing you at any minute."

Another woman railed against the appearance issue by fantasizing, "I knew I should have dressed up to go in, but I didn't have time and I looked like a pear-shaped slob. But I decided to pretend I was one of the understated rich, who don't care about wearing the latest styles. And I felt better."

While women are judging you, they are also judging themselves. This tendency to self-appraise ("Am I dressed right?" "Am I attractive?" "Do I look confident?") can be a hidden threat to your sales approach. As a marketer, your ability to see what she sees in her mirror can help you tailor messages and approaches that are not sabotaged by her own evolving self-esteem. Chapter 5 focuses on this tug-of-war in the mirror so that you can connect with what is inside a woman's head when she evaluates whether your brand fits her self-image.

Lesson 2. Your Service Should Be Democratic Even If the Merchandise Is Not

Realize that women's daily agendas are complicated and that those personal agendas affect when and how they shop and how they look when they do. With women living stressed, multifaceted days that flip back and forth between work and home, they are unlikely to conform to the uniform of your ideal customer. The luxury shopper just came into the Armani boutique in running clothes after a workout. The potential investor happens to have taken a day off to do all her errands and is dressed casually for her, not for you. Just because her attitude is relaxed does not mean her sonar is turned off. Sometimes she is testing you, waiting to be snubbed so that she can be right about you.

Oddly, women sometimes blame themselves for the way they are treated. As one woman told me, "I'm a fairly assertive person, but God only knows what vibes I'm giving off. Maybe I look like I'm intimidated and that's why they act that way."

Landmine 2. Patrolling the Selling Floor

The second landmine is patrolling the selling floor. Once inside a store, a woman begins to check out the lay of the land. Think "gatherer" as well as "hunter" as women move among the racks and the departments, taking in what is on sale, what looks interesting, and where she is likely to buy. Unlike men, who will describe a selling situation as a hunt-get-and-go process, women are checking out everything: the merchandise, the environment, the service, and the salespeople. Call it holistic shopping.

Just Ask Dany Levy, President and Founder of DailyCandy.com . . .

Dany Levy is the founder and president of DailyCandy.com, a national style and trend company whose daily e-mails on "what's hot" attract over 100,000 fashionistas and trend spotters around the country. As a shopping maven, Dany has this description for how women size up a store: "It is interesting to watch the pace that other women shop. I am a very quick shopper. I can walk in and assess the situation in a heartbeat. I can't shop with what I call slow-shopping friends. I do a sort of broad-scope approach and then narrow it down. A lot of women will walk into a store and gravitate toward one item in particular. I think it is just a physiological difference, the same way some women walk into a cocktail party and one sort of takes in the larger picture, and one moves toward the hors d'oeuvres."

That is how women look at the merchandise. How about the way they look at the retail associates?

Who's Selling Whom?

As discussed in the last chapter, with higher-ticket, longer-term decisions such as cars, durable goods, and financial services, women determine whether they have a trusting relationship with the seller. With apparel and household needs, however, women want results more than a relationship. They are in too much of a hurry for the obligations of a relationship.

For example, the process of buying cosmetics is rife with stories of relationship overload. As one woman said to me during a series of interviews about shopping in department stores, "I go there to buy makeup every two months, but I don't go to the same person. I don't want to know their names. I don't want to know who they are. I don't need a personal relationship with them. All I want is for them to make me beautiful and send me home."

Another woman noted, "I don't like pushy salespeople, like if I go into Macy's and they start spraying me. If the product is good enough, it will speak for itself. I don't want someone harassing me when I'm looking." Yet another explained, "When I go shopping, I want to be left alone. But the salespeople are always right there by my side and want to talk to you about it. I don't want to talk about it. I know what I want and I do my research ahead of time, so leave me alone."

Let us relate this to the first lesson in the previous chapter (Know when she is in shopping mode versus deciding mode). **This woman was clearly in deciding mode, and she was not open to any more influence. Did the salesperson hear her when she spoke, or did she pounce? Could you teach your people to believe that women mean what they say?**

However, I have also interviewed women who get annoyed when the shopping experience is purely transactional. For instance, with high-end skin care, women said that they expected the beauty advisor at the counter to "put the product on my face—that personal touch is what I'm paying for." Now, this is the moment when, as a marketer, you may be feeling irritated: "What does she want—contact or not?" As frustrating as it is, try to stop the impulse to scream "Make up your mind" and accept it. She makes the rules and reverses them as she goes along.

As a marketer, I can see how women sometimes give off confusing signals and lure salespeople into believing that they are needed. For example, after all the years I worked in marketing cosmetics and skin care, I am the biggest sucker for accepting an offer for a makeover. Maybe it is because I unconsciously smile when I walk the aisles. Maybe I look like I need some help. I am invariably accosted by someone who says, "Oh, please, let me fix your eyes." More often than not, I let them. Then, out of guilt, I buy at least one of the products they put on me. I guess that women like me are why salespeople never stop trying the "I am your beauty pal" routine. It works with some of us.

Contradicting their desire to be left alone while they shop, women do expect that salespeople will be ready the minute they need them. Women's impatience spikes at the moment it is time to buy: "When you walk into Stern's or something, you kind of have to yell across the counter, 'Excuse me, can you help me!'"

As a retailer or service provider, you can train your people in the art of making direct eye contact while saying, "I'm here whenever you need me," and then stepping away. It is easy to see when a woman wants the salesperson's help. Watch for her eyes to dart around, notice her walking quickly in search of something, and listen for the last straw: "Is there anybody here to take my money?" That's when you should hustle.

Because they like to hear other's opinions before making decisions, women wish that salespeople would be honest: "I feel like they'll tell you, 'Yeah, it looks good!' just to make the sale, so I depend more on friends and catalogs or things like that to get an opinion, or I'll go in with something in mind already." Doing advance reference checks with friends is another indication of the board of director's quadrant at work, as discussed in the previous chapter.

Pay Attention When She Wants Attention

After a woman has assessed the lay of the land, her vigilante attitude kicks in. She is not waiting to be served. She demands it: "I go to people and tell them I need help. I don't stand there waiting for someone to come to me. I go fetch."

In a session on financial services at Just Ask a Woman, one woman coached another woman in retail tactics this way: "If they don't shake your hand, you shake theirs. You don't have to wait, you just reach out and say, 'I'm Mary Smith and this is my husband Joe. He just makes the money. I invest it.'" I hear this kind of assertive remark more often either from women who are higher up on the income and education ladder or from those women with less money who are made vengeful by so many bad retail experiences.

In mass merchandise outlets, where cashiers are scarce and navigation is blocked through overloaded aisles and disorganized merchandise, women's temperatures climb sky-high. Remember the stress? It is still there. And, if a woman is in a high-priced store, her expectations for immediate attention are even higher, such as those of one woman who told me, "If I'm going to spend a lot of money in a jewelry department, I want to be waited on. But you look and look and look and sometimes you can't even find anyone on the floor." And retailers wonder why sales are down.

The experience of retail department stores pales in comparison with that of the automotive and technological industries, in which women rarely feel talked to, let alone respected.

As one woman told me, "I had a hard time getting the salesperson to show me anything other than where the key went. I wanted to look under the hood and see how hard it was going to be to change the oil. They just kept telling me how easy it was to park. Finally, I brought my husband in to see it since his check was paying for it. They started talking to him about maintenance and I'm like, excuse me, I change *his* oil."

Even though women buy nearly 50 percent of all cars and trucks[5] and influence the purchase of many more, women still experience bad treatment compared to men. Rather than resent it, the vigilante shopper takes revenge: "I'm in sales, and I'm a pretty good negotiator, but I appreciate the negotiating skills of a friend of mine's husband. I'll pay him cash to go with me when it comes to negotiating. They'll ask me, 'Is this your husband?' and I'll tell them, 'No, that's who I'm paying to make sure I get the best deal.'"

One unconscious tactic of salespeople is to create a nonexistent or unspoken relationship with customers. Because women are tuned in to the motivations of salespeople, some salespeople try to leverage that seeming intimacy into a bonding opportunity with customers. A few months after the events of September 11, 2001, as New York's retail economy continued to lag, I finally went back to a favorite store. Although I did not know the sales associate who checked me out, she acknowledged my frequent-buyer card. She decided to let me in on what was happening in the store: "Do you believe that *they* are asking us to call all our best customers and ask them why they aren't coming in to the store? I feel embarrassed to do that!"

In her mind, did she think that, as a woman, I would understand and connect with her frustration or feel guilty enough to buy more? On that level, I might. As a customer, however, I wondered just how troubled their business was that they had to drag customers from their homes. How many times have you heard cashiers complaining that they hadn't had a break for hours or that they couldn't wait to get off work? Such comments are part of a bonding strategy—though perhaps an unconscious one—that does a disservice to the store, even if it does make the employee feel that he or she is opening up and being friendly and natural with customers.

Lesson 3. Beware of the So-Called Bonding Behavior of Your Staff

Sales associates sometimes confide their own worries and feelings, particularly to female customers because women appear to be more empathetic. However, the net result of airing all this dirty laundry is that customers may wonder how tough you are on your employees or whether you just hire people who are more concerned with getting time off than with assisting customers. A couple of workmen rode up the elevator of a luxury store where I was shopping. They turned to each other and joked about the cheap quality of the new shelves they were installing on the floors: "That stuff just fell apart," they laughed as they smiled at me. Their remarks made me feel that the store was doing renovations poorly, which reflected badly on the store environment. Being buddies with the construction guys did not compensate for that.

Landmine 3. Nailing the Mission

To understand this third landmine, close your eyes and try to put yourself in the place of the woman in the store. She is carrying a lot of stuff—not only her handbag or briefcase but also the merchandise she has flung over her arms. She is searching for a dressing room, which is nowhere to be found. She would love to find a restroom, but they always seem to be located in the opposite corner, and she is already stretching the time limits of her lunch break. Even if she found one, what would she do with the stuff she has already picked out? Running in heels, she finally tracks down a salesperson. (Remember how the women at the cosmetics counter were all over her on the first floor? Not so upstairs.)

As she waits in the checkout line, juggling bags and clothes, she watches the clerk slowly pecking away at a computer that she seems to have just learned to use that day. Another clerk asks the computer clerk about her lunch break and complains about their boss, and a customer interrupts to ask whether the store carries certain pants in an extra-small size. (Hate her.)

Lesson 4. When She Is Ready to Check Out, She Is Already Checked Out—Hurry!

Whole Foods has mastered the speedy and courteous checkout system. The chain has invested in many, many more registers than has the average food store. The customers assemble in three lines, and a director stands in front, takes a person from each line, and sends them to the next available register. The director keeps things fair, and no one gets confused as to where to go. With so many registers, even a complicated checkout does not keep anyone else waiting. In fact, I understand that the policy is that the checkout may not take more than two to four minutes, even at its longest.

The typical checkout process can inflame the vigilante shopper. She is exhausted, stressed, and so ready just to drop everything on the floor and leave. In fact, many retailers would learn a lot from inspecting the racks near their cash registers. Abandoned, unbought merchandise is a great indicator that a vigilante shopper has just given up and made her getaway without a purchase.

In the airline business, the equivalent of the checkout line is the check-in line. Continental Airlines found a way to get customer information and simultaneously speed in-line waiting time. An agent at their Newark Airport hub worked her way down the check-in line and wrote down the exact time people got into the line. The concept was that this time notation would be matched by a second reading of the time they reached the gate agent to measure how quickly they moved along. As a customer, I appreciated that the agents were appraised based on how fast we made it to the counter. It was like we were all trying to win a contest of customer care.

Another espionage technique that would improve your store's service IQ would be to think of your dressing-room attendants as customer listeners. Women who shop with friends or daughters talk in the dressing room. A lot. And loudly. By listening to their dialogue, you can improve your knowledge of what is on women's minds and what is right or wrong about your store and its merchandise. At Just Ask a Woman, we are still trying to figure out how to do research there or in a ladies' room. It does not get more honest.

The Not-So-Quick Getaway

One woman I interviewed had this theory about the retail conspiracy for customer retention: "I know they are paid to work slow to keep you in the store as long as possible. But when you've got a bus to catch and the cashier is saying to herself, 'Let me sca-a-a-an this, let me sca-a-a-an this' as slow as she can, I'm like, 'SCAN IT AND PUT IT IN THE BAG!' I've got two kids with me and it drives me *nuts!*"

The presence of children on shopping trips is an unavoidable fact of retail life. One of the reasons that both Wal-Mart, Target, and Kohl's are so successful is that they have accepted that women sometimes must bring their children with them when they shop. That is why their aisles are so wide and why their carts are so big with safe seats to hold little ones as well as packages. They want to be stores where women feel free to bring their kids and where kids will want to come.

Paul Higham of Wal-Mart says, "We do our best to make it a kid-friendly environment. Taking children shopping is frequently a reality, particularly on a weekend. If you need to go shopping at a discount store and you know that your kids love the experience, it makes your life so much easier. At many of our supercenter locations, if kids come out on a Saturday morning with their mom, they get a free cookie from the bakery department. Many of our stores have helium-filled balloons for kids. Saturday morning shopping with kids is a reality for a lot of people."

That is not the case in other stores. "It feels like you aren't supposed to have children if you shop there," one woman said about a luxury store. Another noted, "I usually try to shop for kids' clothes without my kids because the last time I left the Gap, I went to another store, and I looked in the stroller and realized that my two-year-old had two pairs of Gap pants in her lap, so we had to return them. Also, a lot of times, if one child starts to scream, they all start, so it gets hectic." (And a little stressed, maybe?)

Kids are part of the retail picture, even for other purchases. For those women who have only the weekend to shop for cars, kids come along for the ride. One of the sweetest, calmest women I ever interviewed described her annoyance with the "I have to ask my manager" pricing negotiations that some dealers endorse. She said, "When I shop, I control my kids. But when I start getting the runaround from salespeople, I don't control them anymore."

Imagine the dealer caught unaware by this mild-mannered

mom turned vigilante shopper while her kids jump in and out of cars, scream around the showroom, honk horns, and leave tiny fingerprints on the dash.

When women reach the state of true frustration, they walk. Unlike the way they may have behaved in the past, when women may have gritted their teeth through a bad sales experience, women are throwing down the gauntlet and taking names.

Lesson 5. She Will Come Back to Stores That Like Her and Are Like Her

At the end of each retail experience, women reach a verdict: Either they return to build a relationship, or they don't. For better or worse, they tell their friends. As discussed earlier in Chapter 3 on decision making, women love to commiserate and punish the wrongdoers. And they will tell as many friends as possible in order to rectify what happened to them.

The clearest determinant of how women relate to your stores is to look at any research you already have in-house for the ratings on an often-asked survey question. Is this a store for me or for someone like me? Women personalize the retail experience to decide whether or not they feel at home. How can you make the shopping experience easier and more comfortable? If a woman says it is good for someone else, she is politely saying, "But not for me."

Never forget that women's lives are extremely stressed and pressed for time. The more complex your buying process, your service rules, and your credit procedures, the less patience she has for you. If she thinks that buying you and your products will further complicate her life, she will find another place to shop. Borrow from analogous businesses. Could you apply a drive-in element to your business? Eckerd and others did when they added pick-up prescription windows to their stores. Cut out the extraneous steps that are really for your benefit, and figure out how to help women buy you easily and get on with their lives. That is what women really want.

Since shopping may seem like a necessary evil, can you find ways to convert it to a pleasurable escape? Some retailers have done this, such as Saks Fifth Avenue, whose new concierge service provides assistants to busy women to act as personal pilots through the store. Another example is furniture retailer Ikea, which provides supervised play areas for kids so that moms can browse kid-free. Some women have told me that they would never trust anyone to supervise their kids, and retailers have shared their fears related to their liability for children's safety. Without some kind of kid diversion, however, many mothers may be heading to the exit door for relief before they have bought your product.

Other retailers realize that they need to overhaul the entire selling model to attract women. Take Nike. Many marketers may consider Nike as an example of a company that already understands women based on its years of female-empowerment advertising featuring athletes like Mia Hamm and Jackie Joyner-Kersee. Surprisingly, however, that imagery did not necessarily translate to sales at the retail level, even when the company created its special Niketown boutiques. As an example, the Niketown store in San Francisco relegated women's athletic wear to the fourth floor, so women had to plow through men's equipment for every possible sport just to find the escalator to the next floor of guys' stuff.

In an article in the August 2002 issue of *Fast Company* regarding the creation of Nike's new women's store, Nike Goddess, author Fara Warner reported that the "feel of the original Niketown store [was] dark, loud, and harsh—in a word, male." She quoted

Nike's designer John Hoke as saying, "I got used to hearing people describe us as brutal, but that's because our initial reaction to selling the Nike brand was to turn up the volume. [Nike] Goddess is about turning the volume down. I wanted people to come in and take a breath."[6]

The Nike Goddess stores were designed as places where women would want to shop. From the same article, Hoke explained, "Women weren't comfortable in our stores. So I figured out where they would be comfortable—most likely their own homes. The store has more of a residential feel. I wanted it to have furnishings, not fixtures."[7] Although sales numbers have not yet been revealed, their plans for expansion are promising.

Making women feel truly at home might seem too ambitious for you, but you can do simple things at least to ease the visit. Look at your basic store policies for credit, exchanges, and returns. I have my own case on the credit limit issue. To maximize points, I use my American Express card for almost everything I buy. But finally I caved in to one department store's pitch and signed up for their store credit card. Now, my credit limit on my Amex card is fairly high by any standards. But after hitting about $1,000 in that store (OK, that is a lot of shopping, but I decided to maximize the extra 10 percent I got off everything for signing up), I hit an embarrassing roadblock. At each subsequent use of the card, the clerk would stare at the computer, pick up the phone, and in a deeply concerned voice ask what my credit limit was. Finally, they cut me off. Not only did I feel like a deadbeat (the imperious look of a 22-year-old associate did not help), but I stopped using their card and instead finished up with my Amex card. Wasn't their goal to get me to spend? I felt like I was being punished for taking their offer.

In addition, retailers have recently been retaliating against return abuses (evening gowns worn to one formal event and then returned) by forcing customers to retain receipts, tags, and other paperwork with tighter time constraints. Women running through insanely busy days are lucky to retain their driver's license, let alone your paperwork.

Customers just want their money back, even if retailers do not want to give it to them. An example of this is the shell game that retailers see in the bridal registry business. The *Wall Street Journal* reported in May 2002 that "couples register for an estimated $10 billion of gifts, and that wedding gifts come back at much higher rates than other merchandise."[8] It seems that cash-strapped newlyweds are making returns with the expectation that the return value will be credited to their credit cards. In retaliation, stores like Neiman Marcus and Tiffany are demanding that they take store credit. The retail relationship ends not so happily ever after. One idea that stores might try is to offer returning customers the opportunity to get a 5 to 10 percent discount on any purchases they make in the store with their store credit. This would at least foster trust in the new relationship with the newlyweds and perhaps generate an even bigger purchase.

How else can you help women feel at home away from home? Is your parking lot well lit and convenient, especially if mom has a baby and stroller in tow? Are the restrooms plentiful, clean, family-friendly, and easy to find? Mobil stations advertise their clean restrooms for the millions of traveling women who notice. Wal-Mart supercenters that feature Quick Lubes brag that they have the world's best waiting rooms. Some car dealerships and service bays are setting up onsite work-friendly, child-friendly areas with computers for waiting moms and TVs and video games to occupy kids. If cell phones do not work in your stores, do you have easy access to public phones so that women can stay connected? (Surely, the expense of installing them is less than the lost revenue when women prematurely leave your store.) Little

---

ADVICE ON WOMEN'S LEADERSHIP

"For most of my 25-year career, I was the only woman. I never thought about being the only woman; I just did the best job I could. I thought of myself as a leader who just happened to be a woman. Over the last three years, I've attended several women's business conferences, and I've been able to network with women that I have a lot in common with, and I have learned that women take their purchases and their buying and their relationships seriously."

—*Bonnie Reitz, senior vice president for sales and marketing at Continental Airlines*

---

things like this can determine whether women relax and enjoy your retail experience or take up arms to attack again. It is your choice.

Cracking the Code on Shopping

1. *Make a good first impression; she is watching.* Remember that women are paying attention to every detail and nuance of your store, even when they are in a stressed-out hurry. Women have amazing peripheral audio and visual abilities. Call it eavesdropping. Call it spying. But know that it is happening, and clean up your act.

2. *Your service should be democratic even if the merchandise is not.* Every retailer or service provider has a marketing reason to differentiate the experience and the merchandise—from discount to prestige. However, there is no reason to differentiate the service once women have entered your store. All your cus-

tomers are moms, daughters, wives, and employees—women with money to spend and desire for respect and attention. Judging by appearance or attitude, or ignoring a woman with screaming kids, is a way to kiss your profits goodbye.

3. *Beware of the so-called bonding behavior of your staff.* Every gesture and every word count. If your employees, even in a gesture of intimacy, decide to air their (or your) dirty laundry, such as seemingly unfair store policies or too much overtime, women will listen and judge you. A woman may smile and sympathize at the shared confidence of your salesclerks, but inside she's thinking, "What about me?" She is your customer, not your pal.

4. *When she is ready to check out, she is already checked out—hurry!* Once a woman has given you her precious time, her first thought is the lengthy to-do list that is constantly scrolling in her head. She has somewhere else to go, and you tarnish a great in-store shopping experience if you ruin the checkout moment. Reducing the number of registers or allowing too many associates to go on break at the key windows for women, such as lunchtime or on the way home from the office, is asking for trouble. Unattended registers make her crazy. She did her job by shopping. Now it is your turn.

5. *She will come back to stores that like her and are like her.* Looping back to the learning from Chapters 2 and 3, women's personal stress and their complex ways of making decisions put a particular burden on retailers and those who market through them. How can you make the buying experience as stress-free and simple as possible? How can you rethink the way you sort merchandise, create an environment, and treat her as a person to ensure that she can enjoy and extend the time she spends with you? Remember that you are not number one on her shopping

list. It is her family. Her needs. Her time. You are there merely to get her where she really wants to go: home.

In the next chapter I explore how your brand can get closer to your female customers by going behind their internal mirrors. This is all about how a woman's looks and feelings about herself influence the way she responds to your products and especially to your advertising and communications.

CHAPTER
5

The Tug-of-War with the Mirror

I could use a catcall now and then.

Think women are tough on retail? Wait until you hear how tough they are on their own looks. Despite all the Oprah episodes, self-help books, and magazine articles on self-esteem, many women continue to critique themselves, and sometimes they think that marketers are doing it, too. For better or for worse, many women are perfectly aware that strangers, including car dealers and drugstore clerks, give them that once-over that she reads loud and clear. Just as the vigilante shoppers of the previous chapter want to be validated as decision makers, women also want to be validated as women, even though they do not admit it: "Does the salesperson think I look pretty enough, savvy enough, or rich enough to shop here? Why do I care what they think?" Indeed, why?

This chapter exposes the tug-of-war with the mirror and examines the hidden emotions that women feel and marketers face when they want to connect to them. Your advertising and communications programs reflect your brand's view of women. Do your ads show that you want women's business? Does the casting in your commercials represent what your female customers relate to or aspire to? Even if you get your product right for women, you will lose her if your imagery communicates "not for me."

A woman's judgment of the women associated with your brand drives the way she responds to you. Why are you using that skinny woman to sell me insurance? Is that computer meant for a teenager or for me? Does that bank think I'm a grandmother? She is not paranoid; she is weighing your message on her internal beauty meter more than you may know.

This chapter includes lessons for the players in the multibillion-dollar beauty industries, such as cosmetics and hair, as well as for their beauty cousins such as weight loss, fitness, and fashion. However, marketers from all business sectors will find surprising insights that will influence the way you judge your advertising and communications to female consumers.

I know these insights from my own experience as a woman and a marketer for Avon and as an agency leader. As the advertising director of Avon's U.S. business, and later as CEO of the advertising agency that won their business, I helped develop their campaigns for cosmetics, skin care, and fragrance. I have worked on every segment of the beauty category, and certainly on every major body part and at every price point, from Jergens hand lotions to Clairol hair color to teen products like Johnson & Johnson's Clean N Clear to salon products like Matrix Essentials Professional hair products and prestige beauty for Estee Lauder Prescriptives and Elizabeth Arden Salons and Spas. My own beauty obsession started when I spent my first paycheck from my college summer job as a bank teller on a tube of black eyeliner from Love Cosmetics.

Because I have had a long relationship with beauty, this is the easiest and yet the most challenging chapter for me to write. I have

---

ADVICE ON MARKETING WITH WOMEN

"In our business there is a passion and an understanding of the business that only women can bring. The emotionalism of buying a lipstick is something lost on most marketers. It just makes you feel good. In our business, you can never discount the emotional side of the equation. I've been asked about a hundred times about what it's like to work with women because I came out of the military, and I worked in giant plants. I enjoy working with women. In my business, women are more knowledgeable; they understand at a deeper level how the product works; and they are passionate about their products. They love using them."

—*Dan Brestle, president of Estee Lauder*

---

spent many years of my career investigating how women feel about how they look. The challenge is to untangle the truths behind her internal mirror because her feelings are so complex and personal. I will share the private thoughts that women are unlikely to reveal to you unless you are a friend or unless you treat them like one, which is what I do when I interview them.

The Mirror Inside

The tug-of-war with the mirror is not just the province of unattractive or insecure women. No matter how beautiful or accomplished, most women harbor doubts about their looks. Here is an example from a recent experience. I had lunch with a friend who is a leader in the advertising business. She is responsible for millions of dollars in revenue from fashion and beauty clients.

We met in a restaurant on a sunny day in Manhattan, and she sighed, "I just walked past one of those really big construction sites where about 50 guys were taking a lunch break. Do you think I got one single whistle?"

I laughed and asked her, "Didn't you flash them a little smile so they'd know it would be okay?" (Kind of a mercy catcall, but it still counts.)

This attractive, slender, chic success story, now 50-plus, was wistful about hardhat whistles gone by, something she used to dread. She knows that she is successful, yet she needs to feel beautiful, too. This personal truth is the kind of thing that women easily confide to friends, but they are not so honest in this area when they are talking to corporations and marketers who want to sell to them. It is easier and less embarrassing to keep those feelings inside.

Inside every woman is a finely calibrated mirror, a woman's internal critic of all the factors of looking good that affect feeling good: youthful looks, fit bodies, fashion sense, reactions from others. When quizzed during market research sessions, women sing the praises of inner beauty. They give the countless rote responses: "What matters is how I feel inside." "Supermodels are too skinny." "I don't look at magazines; I like myself the way I am." In private, however, they admit that looks still count: "Do I look fat in this?" "If only I could lose ten pounds!" "Do you think I look older than she does?" So many women constantly check themselves out in the mirror and compare themselves to other women.

Jen Levine, a colleague at Just Ask a Woman, calls this silent judgment of other women *drive-by makeovers*. Have you ever done it? I confess that Jen and I sometimes do drive-by makeovers while we wait in airport lounges. Some women do them while walking through shopping malls. They see a stranger and immediately conclude, "She should lose the red lipstick," or, "What she should do is cut out that perm and try some highlights." It sounds cruel, but for women it is a cross between being silently helpful and feeling better about their own insecurities. One woman I interviewed admitted that she plays the role of fashion cop: "The important thing is not to wear something just because it's in style if it looks terrible on you. I walk around looking at women saying, 'Glamour don't, glamour don't, glamour don't,' all day long."

Women's compulsion to check out other women led to the blockbuster success of *InStyle* magazine, "one of the most profitable up-market fashion magazines in America," in the words of its "godmother," Ann Moore.

Just Ask Ann Moore, Chairman and Chief Executive Officer of Time Inc. . . .

Ann told me the story of how InStyle *was born based entirely on the premise that women like to look at other women: "How did [publisher] Anne Jackson and I ever get all those men [former leaders of Time Inc.] to approve this launch? A picture is worth a thousand words. It was the week after the Oscars, and we took every Time Inc. magazine and put them on one board and said, 'This is our coverage of the Oscars.' And what we had were very tiny black-and-white pictures from just the waist up of people accepting the awards. That year, Catherine Deneuve was in a black dress with a shocking pink boa. But what you did not see was that it was pink, and that she had shocking pink shoes and a shocking pink purse to match. On another board, we showed all the fabulous kinds of paparazzi photos on the red carpet, and it made the statement that the Oscars were not just about the awards. It was as much about the dresses and the shoes and the purse that goes with everything. Those two boards said more than anything we could have shown them. What drove the success of* InStyle *was the complete addiction of women. Women rip things out of magazines and walk into stores and demand to buy them."*

Women's interest in watching other women is why makeover segments are so popular on TV morning shows and in women's magazines. Women love the before and after of it all. Recognizing this spectator sport has built brands. John Frieda was an unknown British hairdresser until his small, home-made-looking ad for a styling product called Frizz-Ease started to appear in magazines in 1989. The ad showed nightmare frizzy hair on one side of the model's head. The other side had been transformed into silky, shiny, straight locks. By 1991 his products became number seven in sales for all hair care products in drugstores (no small feat given the thousands of entries in this category). The company is still a big player in styling products. Women know the makeover results are exaggerated, but they don't care. It's about hope.

As a marketer, realize that a woman does her own mental makeover with your ads. Billboards, TV spots, and magazine ads offer her hundreds of opportunities to silently conduct the like her/hate her test. This relates to you because she may also be imputing that score onto your brand (for me/not for me). Casting matters to women.

Lesson 1. Cast Your Ads through a Woman's Eyes

Women are judging the women in your ads, so you need to think the same way she does, or at least ask about her reactions to your casting choices (unless your brand is Gucci, where the less likable the model is, the better the brand fit).

Look at any model and ask these questions from a woman's point of view: Does she look happy? Does she smile with her eyes? Does she look slender but healthy? Does she look like she could have a good laugh? Does she seem to have a life? Would you like to have a cup of coffee with her? You can skip this kind of thinking if you want to—but your female customers will not.

As marketers, you may be relying on your agency's creative director to cast your ads. It might be a good idea to check the beauty IQ of your ad agency. There is a dirty little secret that the ad agency community does not like to talk about much: Most agencies' creative directors, particularly of the largest and most influential creative shops, are men. If you look at their TV reels or the reels of award-winning work they admire, you will get a true view of what and who they think is beautiful. Look at the women they cast. Do they reflect real women's values? Are the women likable, funny, warm, and healthy? Or do they look like Central Casting for Models, Inc.—the perfect beer-ad babes that mirror what men like to see in a woman? Whether your creative team is composed of men or women, their reel will give you insights into how they think. The women who appear in your advertising represent who your brand believes women are. Remember that the next time you see the commercial director's choice for the model he or she would like to make a star on behalf of your brand.

The right answer rests with women themselves. Know that women measure themselves against that image. Trust them enough to ask before you shoot. The Gap has resurrected a campaign that was famous for featuring celebrities of every age and style. Beautiful, if now gracefully lined, faces of Sissy Spacek and Marianne Faithful are juxtaposed next to images of Shalom Harlow and Bridget Hall. The implied message that intelligent, discerning women of every age look beautiful in Gap jeans and shirts is not lost on female consumers. Eileen Fisher also runs ads that gather the tall and the short, the svelte and the round, into a panorama of women's beauty that fits her easy-to-wear styles.

Beauty or Self-Esteem?

It may seem shallow to be dwelling on outer beauty when it is so much more PC to talk about inner beauty. Over the past five years or so, women have learned to mask their fascination with physical beauty by shelving it under the umbrella of self-esteem. Once as-sociated with self-confidence, awareness, and pride, this hyphen-ated word has created an entire industry of "feel good, look good, be good" products. The runaway success of Hearst's O magazine from Oprah Winfrey is a testament to women's search for self-esteem. Each year, Lifetime Television dedicates the month of May to self-esteem programming. A Google.com search turned up nearly one million reference hits on self-esteem. There is even a National Association of Self-Esteem. With this halo wrapped around self-esteem, it is no wonder that the beauty industry has embraced the concept. An ad for Chanel's Précision makeup en-courages women to "reveal your true inner beauty." Mascara to help you feel good about yourself. A shot of collagen to restore your confidence. Self-esteem can sometimes be used interchange-ably with vanity.

On one hand, women prize the value of feeling good inside; on the other hand, they play into the media's fixation with traditional outer beauty. Which hand wins? It's a toss-up. If you make the call based on dollars and cents, outer beauty tri-umphs. In 2001 alone, women plunked down $306 million on an-tiaging creams, according to an article in the July 2002 issue of *Marie Claire*.[1] But the struggle over what is beautiful goes on.

Dany Levy, founder of trend and style media company Daily-Candy.com sees it this way: "I think women are becoming more and more self-conscious about their age, their wrinkles, their breast size, their weight. There are two countercurrents. There is the one that is sort of antibeauty, the 'I am beautiful for who I am; I am not going to buy in to any of this propaganda about needing to fit into a C cup or be stick skinny' group. At the same time, there is a group that is open [about plastic surgery], who admit that 'not a part of me is real and I am damn proud.'"

Understanding this struggle between women and the idealized

images they see is key to creating effective messages—not just for beauty businesses but also for any company looking to connect with women. For example, what does this mean if you are a marketer creating a commercial for a luxury car? Since women buy nearly 50 percent of cars and influence the purchase of many more,[2] and since the women with the highest income and the most independent decision-making ability are over 40, it should mean a lot. Just how should the woman in your commercial look? (Be careful that she does not look too young to have made enough money to afford it. And not so perfect that she looks like a trophy wife. But not so mature that you seem to be targeting empty nesters, unless you are.)

You might imagine that the leaders in the beauty business would always be asking their customers, "What's beautiful to you?" However, I have observed that most marketers in the beauty categories (cosmetics, weight loss, fashion, beauty services, wellness, and even luxury goods) already consider themselves wise about what women want. They are sometimes the most limited in their definition of women's aspirations (beautiful, thin, vacuous). Whether it is the hair colorist, the makeup guru, or the designer, many see themselves as *the* self-styled virtuosos of what women want. In my experience from both the agency and client worlds, I have noticed that marketers frequently prefer to listen to themselves, rather than to women. (It's easier, and you always agree with yourself.)

Marketers' understanding of women's internal beauty dialogue deteriorates as you expand beyond the "women's world" of beauty. Even if you sell cars, pharmaceuticals, or insurance, you are not exempt from deciphering this explosive combination of women, their appearance, and their sense of self-worth. How do you cast female models and real women in your commercials and print ads? What are you subliminally or overtly promising when you choose a woman to represent everywoman?

Do you really know how good your customer thinks she looks? How good she really feels? A very successful woman who works with me still pictures herself as she looked in her awkward high school days. To look at her beautiful skin, hair, and body, you would never know what she sees in her mirror. Her friends call her the most secure, insecure person they know.

Beauty, fitness, confidence, and power are all intertwined in women's minds. Understanding these issues can strengthen your brand's relevance to women.

Lesson 2. Play against Type and Get Women's Attention

Pitting fat against thin is a tired joke. Knowing that women are ambiguous about where they rank in the looks hierarchy, you should be cautious about casting the cocky young beauty. A snack-food client showed me an ad concept I convinced them to reject. It featured a young woman taking revenge on a coworker who had gotten a promotion instead of her. While dumping a pile of candy on the coworker's desk, the thin "heroine" muttered that the coworker might have gained the corner office, but she would never fit into a size 6. Women would have considered that heroine to be a villain—not only impossibly skinny, but also a poor loser. All this to sell a snack that is supposed to be good for you.

Move past the stereotypes. Women know that every woman is different. They like to see ads like those from clothing designer Donna Karan, who has often shown a range of ages and looks, or from Banana Republic and J. Crew, which match their clothes to an attitude rather than an age.

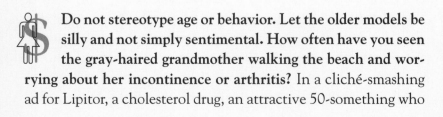 **Do not stereotype age or behavior. Let the older models be silly and not simply sentimental. How often have you seen the gray-haired grandmother walking the beach and worrying about her incontinence or arthritis?** In a cliché-smashing ad for Lipitor, a cholesterol drug, an attractive 50-something who

is described as a size-6 film-award winner trips on the red carpet as onscreen graphics reveal that her out-of-control cholesterol keeps her from being so perfect.

Let pretty young women be funny or a little insecure, even when they look gorgeous. A series of newspaper ads for Women & Co., a women's financial services division of Citigroup, is a case in point. One ad teases about an attractive professional woman who is spending her savings on expensive shoes instead of investments. In another, a pretty young bride takes a divorce in stride and trades up to a home with a great bathtub. In a commercial for Tide, a recently single mom of two kids gets ready for a date. Play against type, and you will get noticed.

Business-to-business and technology marketers have a lot to learn about this. A review of recent ads from the former give the impression that most of their female customers are the only woman at the conference room table in a meeting full of men. She is wearing a bad suit, and she is in a bad mood. From their ads, most tech companies see their female customer as about 26, with funky hair and clothes, tortoiseshell glasses, and a testy look on her face as she figures out the software systems for her cool architectural design office. Huh? Even offbeat is ubiquitous.

ADVICE ON LISTENING

"I have always come from the viewer perspective, I mean, 'I *am* a woman!' I am a woman that has gone through all these different phases that women go through, and I identify with much of what the viewer says. I really feel that women have more in common than differences, and I have always been very sensitive and empathetic when I talk to other women or hear from them."

—*Carole Black, president of Lifetime Television*

Although it may seem politically incorrect to talk about the stock that women continue to place on appearance, it is a reality. Women are stronger, more confident, and more ambitious than ever, but my years of research reveal that they continue to judge themselves by how much they weigh, how pretty they are, and how attractive they are to others. Throughout my interviews, women praise inner beauty but still keep spending on outer beauty. As one woman remarked to me, "On a bad day, I'll go into a department store and go to the makeup counter and say, 'Put whatever you want on me.' I walk out like a new person." Does she need a new eye shadow? Or a dose of confidence?

From Talk to Truth

Getting women to talk about inner beauty is easy—and inspiring. Asking them to admit their feelings about how they look on the outside is not so easy. Their first response is self-deprecating humor, which in interviews is often an avoidance technique.

Many women use humor to assure you that they are not overly proud of their looks. Women are critical of their own beauty (or perceived lack of it), and they love to share personal war stories to empathize with other women. They laugh during most of their conversation with me, which is funny in itself considering that the beauty industry has very little sense of humor when it markets to women.

Knowing how to ask women about this private struggle is important. To get underneath their guard, I asked women around the country this question, "When were you, are you, or will you be your most beautiful?" I thought I would hear a mix of "I was," "I am," and "I will be." Unfortunately, most of them chose the "I was" option.

Their answers started with humorous memories of beauty gone by: "When I was 30 to 35, I was thin. I was happy. I was single." A

35-year-old said, "When I was younger, I had the Farah Fawcett hair, and I used the curling iron. At one point, I had a perm that made me look like Flippo the clown. But it didn't matter because I felt so good about myself then." And another woman in her late 20s told me, "I think when I was the age of 22, I felt the prettiest because I realized I had sex appeal. The way I walked, the way I carried myself—it was just me that made me pretty. But then I did start wearing mascara, so maybe it was the mascara." (The long-running and successful "Maybe it's Maybelline" campaign got its inspiration from this kind of logic.)

Ask your own consumers or the women in your personal life when they felt or would feel the most beautiful. Gulp. Laughter. Silence. Those are the answers you will get, followed by, "Beautiful? I never thought of myself as beautiful," or a joke response. If you are a woman, ask yourself. Did you answer honestly? Or did you substitute, "I was *prettiest* when. . . ."

Beautiful is the killer word. It is easy for women to admit that they are pretty or cute—or even sexy, which is an attitude as much as a look. Beautiful is the gold standard of both looking great and feeling great. Perfect looks are hard enough to achieve, but women pile on the requirement that they also need to feel beautiful on the inside to be truly beautiful. Women have told me that it is hard to feel beautiful when they are unhappy. (I'm not sure men would put the same burden on feeling handsome.)

Maybe I expected more women around the country to say that their most beautiful time was in the present or that their most beautiful years were yet to come only because of my own beauty myth of living in New York City, where there is a nail salon on nearly every corner, Botox and bagel lunch sessions, and the daily sidewalk-runway competition that lures us into believing we are a lot younger and hotter than we really are.

On behalf of the thousands of New York women I have met and worked with in my career in this city, I must point out a geographic twist on their answers to this question. Most of the women I interviewed in New York saw themselves as much younger than their chronological ages, and it was evident in their styles, their attitudes, and their faces. They were willing recruits for the army of hair colorists, personal trainers, yoga masters, and facialists. And intended or not, they dressed alike (similar to teen behavior) in a uniform of Prada bags, sexy mules, and blown-out hair. (Of course, we New York women are proud of our uniqueness.)

For comparison, I found that in Atlanta, for example, the definition of pretty and fashionable was more individualized, more mature, and more colorful and (their word) sparkly. As one woman said, "I'd be furious if I showed up at a party and saw my dress on someone else." In some smaller towns, girls actually register for their prom dresses so that they do not bump into a clone at the dance. Sophisticated merchants observe differences by geography and differentiate their buys to conform to local tastes. Still, many national fashion and beauty retailers play the same note: All women should look younger and—by their choices of models— thinner and alike.

So, wearing my New York blinders, I was in for a surprise when I took this "most beautiful" question on the road. **Most women placed their most beautiful time in the past, even when the respondent was still in her 20s. Many women felt that they would never be really beautiful again.** These women may be comparing themselves to impossible *Cosmo* cover-girl standards or to 17-year-old pop stars (Britney *finally* turned 21). If, as a marketer, you think that this beauty nostalgia belongs only to women over 45, realize that younger women are also looking back to better days. Perhaps, as you read these quotes, you feel the same surprise that I felt. Are your brand associates approving ads showing scrap art of the cast of the HBO show *Sex and the City* as visualizations of your target? Ask them to take a closer look at their customers. The target audience's self-perception should be at the core of your product and message development. Media clichés don't cut it. Listen to the reality of this young woman: "I felt my most beautiful in my college years, 18 to 22. I still look back at that age and wish I were there. You don't have a commitment to anybody. You can be you. And you have the male attention then more than now."

The media pressure to look beautiful starts way before women hit their 20s, even as early as 13. A 2001 *New York Times* article featured a controversy about an ad for the Blousant Breast Enhancement Tablets.[3] Breast enlargement ads were not a shocker in 2001. Because the ad appeared in the fall 2001 issue of *Teen Vogue*, however, the backlash was powerful. In the ad, teenage testimonials linked bigger breast size to increased self-esteem and confidence. Other teen magazines, such as *CosmoGirl* and *Seventeen* turned down the ad as inappropriate for teens. Nonetheless, this is an indication of just how early the standards of beauty are set— and the statistics and stories about anorexia and bulimia in younger women are often attributed to the impossible-to-achieve images admired by even the youngest teens. If your customer is in this group, your responsibilities as a marketer go far beyond the likability of your casting. Your decisions literally can be a matter of life and death. Mothers of these girls are watching you, too.

Getting Married, Having Babies

Being told you are beautiful is one of the keys to believing you are. This is probably why many women are willing to cite their wedding days and pregnancy as the two times when they felt and looked their most beautiful. One woman told me, "I loved being a bride. I don't think the look on my face and the way that I felt could ever be recaptured. What made me feel beautiful was knowing that all those people were there because they loved me."

Wedding-day memories are treasured for two reasons. First, women grow up being told that their wedding will be the most beautiful day of their lives. Second, on that day more than any other, the bride will hear every friend and relative dear to her say out loud, "You look beautiful." A woman's wedding day is the only time when it is socially acceptable for her to admit that she is beautiful.

For that reason, many marketers from wine to insurance to autos to deodorants have used wedding imagery in their ads. When I worked on the Clairol Nice N Easy hair-coloring brand in the early 1990s, we shot a beautiful commercial with a wedding scene. As marketers, you can imagine the extravaganza at the shoot— bride, groom, wedding party, tables of food, band, streaming sunlight, and dancing hordes. The bride's hair looked great. However, in subsequent commercial testing we learned that female consumers were more interested in the story of the pretty bride than in the product itself. Like babies and puppies, weddings sell—but sometimes they are more interesting than your product. Note to self: Focus harder on the product!

When I say that women tell me they look and feel their most beautiful when pregnant, I get a funny reaction from some moms. How could women find beauty in swollen feet, an expanding belly, and exhaustion? Well, for some moms it is a special kind of beauty. As one woman said, "I think women come into their own when they're pregnant. Pregnant women always seem to be smiling with their beautiful flushed cheeks and their shiny hair. I've seen pictures of my mom when she was pregnant with both my sister and with me, and she just looked more content than I've ever seen her." Another agreed, saying, "I have five children, and each time I was pregnant, I think I was at my most beautiful. My husband would agree with that, and I think he'd also say, 'And when you're asleep.' It has something to do with the mouth being shut."

Pregnancy also comes with permission to say you are beautiful, yet it is rare for a cosmetics company to use a pregnant woman in an ad. I have seen them often in nutrition pitches for orange juice and cereal. A current ad for State Farm Insurance Bank shows a beaming pregnant woman kissing her other small child in a pitch for a "mortgage that gives you more family room." In 2002, pregnancy finally crossed the beauty advertising barrier with ads for Burberry Touch fragrance and Olay Body Wash featuring gloriously huge bellies. These are rare examples of tapping into women's beliefs about the true beauty of being pregnant.

Nearly two thirds of American women get married, and most of them have children. Beauty marketers might look to the beauty of these women's lives instead of clinging to the single, childless images for their brands. It is ironic that many of the supermodels in cosmetic ads are actually married with children. Showing that side of them might increase their appeal to the women to whom you are trying to sell.

The one-dimensional view of models has led to celebrities usurping their place on magazine covers. As Ann Moore, who has overseen *People* magazine for over 10 years, said to me, "Models come in one shape and size, and they have an unhealthy lifestyle. Celebrities come in all shapes and sizes, ages, ethnicity, whatever—they are more real. We think we know them, and even the ones we hate, we are kind of interested in them. There is more authenticity to covering their lives. And celebrities have all sorts of problems. Women can relate to that."

As a marketer, you may be in a position to decide about the use of a celebrity for your brand. While you may want to eliminate women with serious lifestyle issues that conflict with your brand's image, do not shy away from celebrities who have experienced life's inevitable problems, such as divorce or illness. Women empathize with other women who have had a rough ride, especially those who have overcome adversity.

Not Just a Pretty Face

Hair, skin, and clothes are not the only factors. Women also demand a beautiful body. While you may think of a healthy body as being strong and functional, women—especially younger women—equate *healthy* with *thin*.

A 24-year-old responded, "I feel the healthiest [read: thinnest] right now because two of my friends are getting married and I'm the maid of honor, so I need to look like a *Baywatch* babe." Another woman said she felt healthiest at her "Club Med spring break vacation. I was 16, 92 pounds, with long hair, perfect skin, and no worries. And I was comfortable wearing a bikini."

When did thin become a synonym for healthy? Thin is what women see in their internal mirror when they say "healthy." Young women's overly high standards for thinness have fueled the diet and nutrition industries.

As a marketer, how do you deal with this schizophrenia regarding the supposedly ideal body? Slimfast found a way to do it without the too-thin casting problem by filming a commercial from the camera's point of view, showing only a woman's feet and lower legs on a scale. Throughout the spot, the woman, whose face and body we never see, sheds various clothing items to get the scale number down, until she finally whips off her toe ring. That image was a fresh way of acknowledging the issue without leaving the average woman out in the cold.

Another marketer, Mass Mutual Financial Group, avoided the issue of casting perfection by telling a story *for* women but without images *of* women. The commercial invited women to consider their insurance and investment products but featured only a frog. Set against rocker Joan Jett's song "I Hate Myself for Loving You," a large frog appeared on screen, and moving type told the story of her life. "There was a girl who used to play dress up, wanted to be a princess, went to high school, wanted to be Joan Jett, went to college, went blonde, then blue, then purple, got practical, got a job, bumped into a glass ceiling, started her own business, never kissed a frog, never had to." This lead to their tagline, "You can't predict. You can prepare." The commercial was totally engaging and relevant without visually typecasting the young female target.

In the beauty industry, Clinique has run a campaign that has made its mark without a single face. The company's ad for its three-step skin regimen, sold through a visual of a simple toothbrush and the line "Twice a day," is the epitome of talking straight with wit, intelligence, and style. As Dan Brestle, president of Clinique's parent company, Estee Lauder, noted, their simple three-step ad, now nearly 25 years old, is "probably the most successful cosmetics campaign in history because it molded not only the first real major skin care business in U.S. department stores, but guided the consistency with white lab coats and all the other good things at the counter."

Lesson 3. Be True and Talk Straight

Stop tiptoeing around the issues. Try talking to women in straight or even fun language, instead of in the typical condescending and silly beauty-voice tone. Observe the way the women talked in my interviews—in everyday words, with emotional and personal references. That would be a surprise in the beauty category. I believe that beauty companies like Origins and Philosophy pioneered the naming of products using plays on words and frank language, such as Origins' Peace of Mind lotion or Philosophy's Hope in a Jar skin cream and Message in a Bottle shower gel. Hair-care companies took the hair look that women hated most and brought it to the forefront as a desired look, such as TIGI's hair-styling product Bed-head and Charles Worthington's Big Hair.

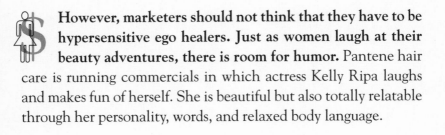 **However, marketers should not think that they have to be hypersensitive ego healers. Just as women laugh at their beauty adventures, there is room for humor.** Pantene hair care is running commercials in which actress Kelly Ripa laughs and makes fun of herself. She is beautiful but also totally relatable through her personality, words, and relaxed body language.

Is She Real or Is She Beautiful?

As women age, marketers become even less sensitive to their feelings about their looks. Many fuel that insecurity with glossy images of gorgeous, skinny 19-year-olds selling everything from anti-wrinkle creams to cellulite reducers. Ironically, no matter how many more cosmetic dollars are spent by 40-year-olds than 14-year-olds, the major beauty companies stick to one supposedly perfect look. She is barely out of college. Her skin is flawless. Her body is swimsuit perfect. She hasn't got a clue, but, boy, she looks great.

In my career, I contributed to some of these images while working on ads for Avon, Clairol, and Johnson & Johnson skin care. Our teams valiantly tried to be more balanced in our model choices, to look for women who were not just vacuous mannequins but showed a semblance of character behind the beauty. I must confess, however, that the models we photographed were knockouts by any standard. During the late 1980s and throughout the 1990s, using images that were not cookie-cutter perfect was a huge departure from the category rules.

Like my peers, I had heard women in focus groups complain that they were annoyed and insulted by the youthful faces and bodies that touted makeup and skin care products. So, while working on the Avon account in 1995, our creative team at N.W. Ayer

& Partners decided to fight the formulaic beauty standard. We assembled a stack of pictures of real women who had a couple of wrinkles, graying hair, or a not-so-perfect nose or body. In fact, according to a *USA Today* poll conducted in spring 2000, the average American woman is a size 14, and her shoe size is a 9. We expected a big round of applause when we showed these photographs of real women to female consumers. We waited. And waited.

After all their cries of "Show us real women!" these consumers looked at us and laughed: "I'm not going to spend $50 on a product to look like her! She's old." When it came down to it, women wanted to see pretty, young faces. Surprisingly, even though women know that beauty marketers are faking them out with dewy, perfect models who do not even need makeup, they would rather participate in the illusion (even when it is not reflected in their own mirrors).

Men are not the only ones who like to look at beautiful women. Many women do, too. Look at the success of Victoria's Secret. Their models define the ultimate in sexy, female beauty. CBS, which has a strong orientation toward families and older viewers, signed on to televise the 2002 Victoria's Secret Fashion Show. The strategy was to make the station seem sexier. As with *Sports Illustrated*'s swimsuit issues, men were a key audience. But women watched, too. Even as we roll our eyes (or sneer) at the perfection of the models, it is about observing, comparing, and measuring the self against an ideal.

Several times when riding in a plane, I have noticed women reading guy magazines like *Maxim*, probably to check out the nearly naked (female) superbodies. (Or trying to figure out what men want.) Their internal dialogue as they peruse through the magazines probably goes something like this: "Wow, she is unbelievable. But those can't be real. I wish I had her arms. I could if I had a personal trainer and had nothing to do but work out all day. My legs are just as long. She's not so great." Observing the details, comparing the ideal to the self—mental makeover complete.

Revlon took up the real woman versus model crusade again in 2001, abandoning its long history with supermodel Cindy Crawford. (Was she too beautiful or too old?) The company made the case that women wanted to see real women for a change. The response to their real-world models? Women yawned. (And the agency was fired.) Revlon is still struggling to stay alive, but Halle Berry kicked off a return to celebrity in late 2002. Note that she is an actress with her own real-life struggles, not a model.

All this is not to say that women are brainwashed. They are practical. What are you selling? What am I getting for my money? Yes, Charles Revson's "hope in a bottle" still plays a role. In this new century, though, the beauty industry is about results in a bottle. Over the past decade, product technology has improved, so women expect performance. Beyond that, especially once women hit 40, they insist on recapturing that most beautiful time they once had.

If you are selling skin care, women want to see flawless skin. That is what they paying for. If you are selling sneakers or insurance, get real. No matter what your category, however, there is a freshness to finding models who look human—and even smart—as well as gorgeous.

How do you combine real and beautiful? I tested an ad for the Chevy Tahoe that showed a woman taking out the third seat of her SUV and carrying it across a mountainside. Women accepted the premise because the model—a tall, strong, attractive, and beautiful woman—looked real: "She looks like she picked that big seat up easily, the way she walks, the way she's dressed, I can relate to that." This model was as gorgeous as any, yet her loose hair, simple makeup, casual clothes, and—more than that—her confident, no-nonsense gait connected with women.

Another way to get real is to pay attention to the details.

When I tested some ad concepts for a low-calorie entree, I was intrigued by just how vigilant the women were about the model's precise body shape: "Her waist looks a little too tiny to be that old." "Wow, if she can run that fast, she must be in unbelievably good shape." "Why is she acting so smug about her weight?" All these comments reveal that women check their personal mirrors when they look at other women in advertising. Casting is only the first step. Choose wardrobe appropriate to the situation and the product. (Can she run in those heels? Does she look like a real mom or a cranky model forced to hold a kid?) Let her environment reflect a little more complexity.

40 (non)Plussed

Baby boomers are heavier consumers of cosmetics than are younger women according to a 2000 survey by the Global Cosmetic Industry. That year, 42 million women over the age of 44 were predicted to purchase cosmetics, compared with 27 million young adults.[4] Nevertheless, the beauty industry looks at these older women as a niche at best.

I have been in many advertising meetings where people have commented that XYZ product is for older women, "you know, past 35." In an interview I did with two friends in marketing, one 42 and the other 47, one commented, "The marketing targets all seem to stop at 35. I'm not even on the grid. What happened to us? Did we just disappear? They send us straight to AARP, and they think we're in nursing homes!" The other friend responded, "And I hate the way they talk about celebrities like Renee Russo or Sharon Stone. 'They look great *for their age.*'"

Despite the best efforts of the self-esteem brigade, women's unspoken standards for outer beauty are stuck somewhere short of age 30. Lipstick commercials are not the only culprits. The casts of nearly every sitcom and feature film are also responsible. It's Jennifer and Cameron and Drew. These media glamour girls set the bar, particularly for teens and young women (although my 50-year-old catcall friend was not immune). And these images shape responses when women think about when they felt or would feel the most beautiful.

Thankfully, though, a ray of light dawns on many women sometime after they hit 40. Women keep seeking beauty and thinness, but the experience of aging raises their appreciation of what is inside. Although traditional outer beauty never really leaves women's radars, their inner-beauty quotient increases with age. Consider these comments from women between the ages of 35 and 54: "It's a confidence that I feel. A voice. The confidence that I know I'm beautiful inside. And that somehow, that's going to radiate to the outside and someone's going to see it." In the words of another woman, "I feel the older I get, the wiser I hope I am, and the more that I feel I need to take care of myself. Twenty-seven was great, but 44 feels beautiful."

The outer-beauty women aren't giving up either. As one said, "You might as well try to look good as you are aging because you don't have any alternative. You go out and get the facials and you get your hair done and spend the dollars because you want to, and if it means a nip and a tuck, I say, girls, do it."

As for their aging bodies, 40-plus women start to replace the ideal of thin with the desire to be fit and energetic. As women age, they start to refine their sense of what is ideal to what is the "real me" they see in the mirror. While a woman's "real me" is not as thin as her earlier ideal, this secret body image is the best version of herself that each woman can hope for. Her "real me" can fit into the tight jeans that she refuses to throw away. (At least, that is her rationale for keeping them for the past four years.)

A practical optimism kicks in as women believe that they can regain their well-being through exercise and weight control, despite the misplaced comments from others. In a recent conversation, a 42-year-old told me, "I used to take it for granted, and now I know I have to work out. If not, I'll start to look old. I went bike riding with a younger friend who was rollerblading, and she said, 'Wow, your butt looks really good for a 42-year-old.' I was shocked she said that. It's that constant reminder that she's younger."

During one interview, a 40-plus woman turned to the entire group and said, "I felt healthiest about a year ago when I ate fruits and vegetables and walked an hour a day. I don't know about anyone else, but we're all at the age to have a midlife crisis, so now is the time we all want to make changes." Another 40-plus woman said, "I feel healthiest now because some friends and I just started a nutrition group, and for the first time I'm not dieting, I'm changing the way I live." Smart marketers can acknowledge this shift from dieting to healthy living by supporting women with products and offers that feed her goals. Special K cereal has offered discounts on high-quality Pilates exercise tapes as a promotion for the brand. In addition, in a nod to the reality that women talk a good game but postpone actually eating healthier, they created a two-week Special K challenge that promised the potential of a six-pound weight loss in exchange for eating two meals of cereal every day for two weeks. Commercials played straight to the couch potato with good intentions.

Promises, Promises

Just like New Year's resolutions, women make a lot of farfetched promises or deals with themselves to get in shape and take care of their bodies. Perhaps they set themselves up to fail and justify the failure as due to difficult life events and responsibilities for others. Women link their diet plans to changing their lives ("I'll get back in shape when I get divorced, my kids go to college, I go on vacation, etc.") rather than to specific pledges ("I will lose ten pounds in the next three months").

Marketers in the nutrition and weight-loss category would be smart to recognize the running start that women need, at least in their minds. So often, the typical weight-loss commercial starts with the "I was about to give up" angle. In reality, many women first have a change of heart, and perhaps have taken a few action steps, before they are ready to hear about a serious weight-loss or eating plan.

Food and diet marketers could help a woman achieve her body goals if they thought the way she thinks: in incremental possibilities, like the nicotine patch in which the dosage tapers down as you succeed. Instead of going for the sweeping before and after, Weight Watchers could talk about getting off the first five pounds, then the next five. Special K's promotion did just that. Whether the idea of eating cereal twice a day was appealing or not, it was simple to do and to remember—and six pounds is a huge jumpstart for many women.

For many women, feeling beautiful goes hand in hand with feeling confident, which in their 40s translates to confidence in the workplace, respect from other women, and appeal to men. However, truly regaining unlined faces and tight bodies is a tougher (and more expensive) challenge. The boom in cosmetic surgery is a testament to the lengths to which women will go to look good. In fact, in a RoperStarch survey conducted for the AARP, 60 percent of women said that they would have cosmetic surgery if it were free, safe, and undetectable.[5]

Lesson 4. Remember the Power of the 40-Plus Market

Recognizing this dichotomy between acceptance of fading beauty and the optimism of fighting aging gracefully is valuable to anyone communicating to women over 40. Do not promise her that she will look young. Instead, invite her to take back the control of her vitality, energy, and strength. She can feel young, and that is an easy sell because self-loving baby boomers feel young, no matter what their age. (I have convinced myself that I am 32 inside.)

Marketers like Disney have done this by touting vacations that adults want to go on to feel like kids without the kids. One of the Gap's recent ad campaigns featured the 50-plus singer-songwriter Carole King and her 20-something daughter, who praises Carole as her role model, making Carole (and, by implication, the millions of boomer women who remember and love her) cool by association.

In an article I wrote for the April 2002 issue of *More*, a magazine dedicated to women over 40, I invited several ad agencies to create ads to convince marketers that women over 40 are powerful, vital consumers—not only in their purchasing power but also in how they see themselves. One saucy ad from D'Arcy LA proclaimed, "At 42, I still kick butt. I just do it in a more expensive shoe." Remember the ad from DiMassimo Brand Advertising mentioned in Chapter 2—"stop showing me pictures of my daughter in underwear"? So few ads adopt that kind of straight-talking attitude that women feel.

In the months following the publication of that article, women wrote dozens of letters to the editor, such as, "It actually brought tears to my eyes when I thought about the value of experience and the beauty of 40-plus women, which is so frequently overlooked in our society." Women in their 40s have a rich sense of humor and memory about the beauty dos and don'ts they have survived. Have fun with them and respect them, too.

Whether they are over 40 or under, women like to be told they are beautiful since that judgment is supposed to come from someone else's lips. A compliment would go a long way—even a compliment from a company.

> ### Just Ask Jim McCann, Chairman and CEO of 1800Flowers.com . . .
>
> *Having built a business from a handful of florist shops to a nearly billion-dollar multichannel flower and gift enterprise, Jim McCann knows the power of what an expression of love can do:* "After 26 years in the business, I am still knocked out by the magic we can create. It's a special connection, an emotion it releases in people. So, if your office manager Kelsey gets flowers in your office, at least a dozen people are going to say, what was that about? At least a dozen times, she gets external stimulation. She is going to have those positive feelings that increase every time. 'Who is it, Kelsey? Whom are you special to?' All those emotions are reinforced and it builds. That's why it's so nice to give flowers to a woman, especially in a public place." *It is interesting to note that the greatest givers of flowers (living compliments) are women. Jim attributes it to* "a DNA variation that makes women more expressive."

Every once in a while, I meet a woman who actually hears compliments from the people she loves. A woman told me, "You know when you look your absolute worst, when you just feel awful, and your husband looks over at you and says, 'You're beautiful.' They just throw those out at you every once in a while, and you think, wait a minute, I know why I married you."

Unfortunately, many women get more criticism than compliments: "I look in the mirror every morning and say, 'Oh, yeah, I've got that glow again.' And then my son will say, 'Uh-oh, you really need to work more on that, Mom.'"

A 28-year-old told me, "I felt more beautiful when I was 21, when I first started going to a bar scene. People were complimenting you even if you weren't beautiful. I probably look just about the same now as I did then, but I felt prettier then. I think it's because I was hearing it more."

Lesson 5. A Compliment Goes a Long Way

Being told you are beautiful by someone you love or believe in is an amazing beauty benefit. Why are no marketers using it? Women could easily squeeze a little flattery into their busy days. Beauty brands might consider finding a way to include the power of a compliment in their advertising. Ponds puts itself squarely on mature women's sides with its campaign for Dramatic Results moisturizer: "My laugh lines got their start in a college dorm at 3 A.M.; my laugh lines have lived through disco (twice)." The compliment is implied through the close-up of a woman laughing, despite her fine lines.

Last Thoughts on Casting

Given the power of this tug-of-war between inner and outer beauty and given the variances of women's feelings as they age, why are images of women so narrowly pictured in ads? Always young, slim, bright, and confident? That decision rests squarely with you, the marketers and your ad agencies. Often, the casting of the women is an indication of what appeals to the creative director of the agency or the director of the commercial, who, more often that not, is a man. Casting is based on what the so-called experts perceive to be beautiful. Unfortunately, in my experience those judgments are Rorschach tests for the look of the women they might like to date, versus the aspirations of the women they are selling to. When brand managers allow commercial directors to have their way, they may learn after the rough cut that their brand is personified by someone their customer hates.

 The solution to the advertising problem does not require that only women create commercials about women. Whichever gender the writer or art director may be, the

job is to understand what is in the consumer's mind, to appreciate where she is in her beauty continuum, and to speak to her in her language and pictures. The director must recognize how women respond to other women in advertisements. Women in my research are asking themselves, "Do I like her or believe her, or is she anyone I'd want to be or know? How do I compare?" This all happens in an instant, but if she mentally checks the "stupid, perfect, witless model" box, she will be skeptical about the rest of what you have to say.

Cracking the Code on the Tug-of-War in the Mirror

1. *Cast your ads through a woman's eyes.* Even though you have lots of experts on your team, including stylists, makeup artists, and casting directors who will tell you that a certain model is *the* look for you, be sure that you are not buying into aspiration that is really unreachable—or worse, undesirable for your target. Give female consumers some credit, and invite them into exercises and photo sorts where they can show you what they believe is—and is not—beautiful.

2. *Play against type and get women's attention.* Real women do not conform to cover-girl stereotypes. Think of the women in your life—your friends, coworkers, family members. The more time you spend with women, the more you will learn how surprising they can be. The plain girl laughs wildly. The glamorous next-door neighbor is a cleaning maniac. The serious executive can dance the merengue. Let your images of women reflect real-world diversity.

3. *Be true and talk straight.* If you are struggling or wary of choosing one woman to represent all women in your advertising (you should be), challenge your creative team to connect with

women in fresh ways. Language that connects because of its truth and symbolic visuals that contain the depth of the message in a simple way can lead to executions that give women room to put themselves in your picture.

4. *Remember the power of the 40-plus market.* The U.S. population is growing older and will continue to do so for the next 20 years. Millions of women turn 40 every day. Start getting to know your biggest customer before it is too late, and look at her the way she sees herself. She is not her mother—not in her appearance, her desires, her income, or her readiness to choose a new brand.

5. *A compliment goes a long way.* A compliment does not mean just telling a female customer that she is pretty. It means recognizing that her self-esteem is connected in her mind with both confidence and appeal to others. If you are selling financial services, recognize that she is already a savvy investor who just might want an edge. If you are marketing insurance, realize that she is an attractive and energetic wage earner, not a needy, worried victim. If your business is food, assume that she knows what your product will or will not do for her, and get to the merits of what makes you special.

This chapter took you behind a woman's internal mirror and showed what happens when her appearance comes between her and your brand. When technology comes into the picture, her invisible power is truly turned on. Log on as she gets intimate with technology in the next chapter.

CHAPTER 6

Intimate with Technology

He asked me to marry him on my voicemail.
I e-mailed him back 'no.'

Right up front I want to admit that I am not a techno queen, but I am an addicted user. I did not go online until 1998, but once I did, I quickly became an eager e-mailer. I got a Palm Pilot a couple of years ago, which has been a real boon since I used to jot down important dates on a piece of paper towel. I am on my second Sony VAIO laptop, which I adore because it is so light I can travel with it painlessly, and its lavender shell looks extremely chic in my lap. I have done my share of online shopping, research, Googling, and daily horoscope checking. In addition, I cannot ride in a cab without checking my voice messages. Here is where I draw the line, though: I do not know my own cell phone number because I do not want anyone to call me on it. That would make it as nasty as a beeper, which is one step away from a leash, in my opinion. The numberless cell phone is my way of retaining control. I guess it is about getting my way on the information superhighway.

I am not alone. Many other women confess to a lukewarm love affair with technology. While some women are just learning to e-mail and others live for their BlackBerries, most women fall into a conflicted intimacy with technology. They love technology for its increasing ability to connect them with the people and places of their lives. They cherish the systems and products that simplify their hectic days. They enjoy the newfound ease of shopping, research, and customer service. As with any new love in their lives, however, they sometimes feel disappointed or, worse, invaded by its insensitive and persistent behavior (like a date who calls too often).

I have interviewed hundreds of women about technology, and here are their concerns: "Even if I want to hide from people, they can find me." Another woman warned, "If they know you are connected, they want a piece of you." Women's fears of too much contact relate to the pressures they already feel in their busy agendas. As one woman said, "There is so little patience for your not being available. We have a fast-food mentality. Get it now. Have it now. Do it now." The stress filter I discussed in Chapter 2 is at work here big-time.

As a marketer, you should know that the efficiency of replacing human contact with digital contact does not always satisfy a woman, even if it saves costs for you. She wants to feel connected but also in control. In this chapter I define technology using the language of an on again/off again relationship, which may differ from the way marketers commonly think of it.

The insights in this chapter provide implications for the way marketers use technology to sell, communicate, and bond with women. Included is straight talk from women about interacting with 800 numbers, researching information, and shopping online. Whether you are a bricks-and-mortar brand or a virtual business or simply use technology to enhance your distribution, you will discover how a woman-smart technology strategy can improve your customer relationships. I will also confront you with how she feels when technology gets too intimate and risks driving her away from your brand.

In the last chapter I revealed how the complications of women's feelings about their appearance can affect your brand communications success. Technology takes her looks out of the equation. She can be sitting at the computer with curlers in her hair, and you would not know it. She can be invisible (eavesdropping in chat rooms) or anonymous (on your site as a nonregistered user). She can find you whenever she wants. She can comparison shop for products in an instant. And if you tick her off, she can zap you, delete you, or simply hang up. Think of it as virtual vigilantism.

Even with its frustrations, most women have welcomed technology into their lives. The numbers tell the story. A June 2001 Nielson Net Ratings survey declared that the number of women online had grown to reflect their representation in the population, to 51.7 percent of active Internet users.[1] More women than men (58 percent vs. 42 percent) had joined the online consumer population in the two years prior to the 2001 America Online/Roper ASW Cyberstudy.[2] What are they doing online? In April 2002 Jupiter Media Metrix reported that 40 percent of all Internet users did research and homework-related projects, whereas 29 percent of moms say they play games online and 29 percent use it to download music.[3] Women are also the decision makers on the hardware itself, spending over $20 billion on home electronics.[4] A *Parenting Magazine* survey in 2000 confirmed that 89 percent of consumer electronics purchases were made or influenced by women.[5]

Why are so many women in love with technology? Contrary to what you might think, the reason is not the amazing inventions, the new gadgets, or the check-in-every-second-with-your-office "benefit." The answer is directly related to technology's ability to simplify, control, and destress their overly agenda-filled lives. In a 1998 *USA Today* article that asked women to rank the top life-improving benefits of technological advances, 91 percent cited timesaving household devices. (When I asked a group of women about their favorite piece of technology, one woman declared, "I thank God for my microwave!") Additionally, 79 percent named the ability to work from home, tied with 79 percent who favored the ability to shop online.[6] Simplify, control, and destress—the keys to her heart.

ADVICE ON INNOVATION

"Well, from a company point of view, we are on the Internet because two young women who work for us said that they had been
playing around with this new technology and that we better look
into it. I said, 'OK, here's $20,000. Let's see if we can get our toe in
the water. That was 1990.'"

—Jim McCann, Chairman and CEO of 1800Flowers.com

Playing Hard to Get

As I have interviewed thousands of women over the past three
years, no matter what the subject (beauty, money, home decor,
health, kids), women turn the topic to technology and how it
helps or hurts the buying process. This chapter presents the helpful aspects, such as well-designed websites, responsive customer
service lines, and the brands that have integrated their communications across all media. First, here are a few speed bumps along
the information highway.

For example, with women as such key users, why is technology
advancing in ways that many women do not care about? Today's
cell phones not only handle e-mail but also can shoot and store
digital photos. The new 2002 BMW 745 is so highly computerized
that even car experts grumble that they need a doctorate to program the radio. With emerging interactivity, women will be able
to order the sweater that Patricia Heaton wears on *Everybody
Loves Raymond*. How many women are dying to do all this? Marketers who use technology to connect with women need to recognize the role it can play in women's day-to-day lives (rather than
invention for invention's sake). Do technology marketers and de-
velopers behave like a lifelong lover or like a one-night stand?

Using technology is one thing. Buying it is another. Many
women agree that one of the least fun things to shop for is con-

sumer electronics. One reason is the merchandise itself, which has so many minute (and, to women, meaningless) variations. The other is the distribution channel. Electronic stores are typically staffed (manned, should be the word) with clerks who are either too into tech or untrained, seemingly low-interest hourly workers. Women are looking for a Sherpa, and instead they get an order taker who is trying to take down the 5 million digits of the product code and your life history so that the form can be chewed up by the register and sent to the loading bay.

I spoke on a panel at the P.C.Forum, an elite high-tech conference sponsored by Internet guru Esther Dyson. It was frightening enough to be wedged onstage between Sun Microsystems' tech genius Bill Joy and interactivity leader Mitchell Kurtzman, talking about how the technologically endowed appliances of the future will communicate with each other. (Will my toaster be asking my refrigerator for a couple of slices of rye?) The scarier thing was listening to questions from the audience, many of whom hearken from the far-forward frontiers of tech exploration. One man stood up to show us something he had designed, a cross between a cell phone and a computer (or was it a light switch?). Then he asked how he could sell this to women through an electronics chain. His explanation of how the device worked was confusing at best. I said to him, "Don't worry about how to explain this to women. First, you'd better figure out how to explain it to the revolving door of part-time employees at Circuit City. If you can't make it easy, forget them. And women, shopping in a rush, will never be as patient or polite as I am sitting up here."

A survey of 1,000 women by electronics store Cambridge Soundworks and its sister online site HiFi.com indicated that 53 percent of women feel intimidated when they buy consumer electronics.[7] To counteract that issue, the two companies partnered to develop a marketing-to-women program called HerHiFi.com that incorporates a special customer service guide called "Ask Kate." The idea was that the fictitious Kate would decode the buying process without the high-tech jargon and focus on gee-whiz extras that men seem to enjoy. This idea might benefit some of the bigger players.

Women tell me that when men are shopping for electronics, they are mostly concerned about what it does and what the next, coolest thing is. Women want to know how it will fit in their lives and their homes and how it will serve not only their needs but also those of the rest of their families. A woman is more interested in checking out the handheld device that her best friend uses than being the first on her block to own something. Remember the board of directors from Chapter 3? She is more likely to listen to the woman with whom she carpools than to the stranger at the counter with a pocket protector.

One woman had this to say about the Mars-Venus difference: "My husband is a total computer geek. He's always changing our computer. He brings home one new hard drive after another. I'm saying, 'Please leave it alone.' But he's constantly getting new stuff." Women shop the electronics aisle with purpose, rather than pleasure, so marketers should support in-store selling that gets to the point of how technology can help connect her life. Unfortunately, that does not happen in many electronics departments.

While the salesperson is explaining the fourteen fabulous downloadable features, she wishes he would just stick to the basics and let her hold the digital camera or the iPod to see how light and hand-friendly it is. Whether hardware or software, women want to know how it fits functionally and aesthetically in their lives.

Lesson 1. The Best Technological Advancement Is the One That Eases Her Life

. . . not the one that you invent or apply just because you can. If you recognize how stressed and pressed for time women are, you will see that your use of technology could speed up the distasteful things and give her more time to enjoy what she enjoys. That is why automated bill paying and e-tickets that reduce workload and waiting time are successful. As one woman said, "I love our PC because we use it for banking, and it keeps me from standing in long lines with the teller." These are example of using technology the right way. Being put on hold for an hour with your Muzak is not productive.

Of course, once women buy the computer or cell phone or the computer-brained dishwasher, the next hurdle is getting tech support when it breaks. Meet a woman's worst enemy: oh-so-unsupportive tech support.

Just Ask Liz Dolan of Satellite Sisters . . .

Formerly global marketing director for Nike, Liz Dolan's current title is second-oldest sister because she cohosts a radio show called "Satellite Sisters" with her four real-life sisters. She has also spun off a website, creating a brand about women's friendships. Dolan told me that she did a program about the "totally humiliating" process of calling tech support: "We actually did a segment about how much we hate tech support. Once you get over your anger at being on hold for an hour and a half, someone is asking you questions you don't know the answer to because you are not a technologist. You just use e-mail, or you just type, or you do your monthly bills on Quicken, but you don't know how it really works, any more than you know how your phone works. The first thing they do is to ask if you have this feature or that. Why would you know that? You have the humiliation of not knowing the answer to most of the questions they ask. And then you get the condescension because you don't know the answer. It's all around the most unfulfilling experience in a person's life, I think."

Some companies have succeeded in creating responsive customer service websites. My colleague Jen Levine lost the cap of the stylus for her Palm Pilot. She e-mailed the company asking how to get a replacement. Their answer: "Certainly. What color would you like?" Maybelline Cosmetics will track down favorite lipstick shades and recommend replacement colors that replicate obsolete products. Technology can work as a friendly customer helper if it is programmed in concert with women's real-life needs.

I've Got Your Number

One of the inventions that fits naturally into women's lives is the cell phone. Thanks to women, cell phones continue to proliferate. Cell phones are becoming the personal networks of women, especially moms who need to stay in touch with their families.

When we conducted some research on technology for a client, one woman who waited for us in the lobby of the hotel was talking on one cell phone and listening on another. Another woman told this story: "I have four pagers: one for each teenager, one for my office, and one for my husband. At night, I put them all in a basket next to my bed, and sometimes the basket is jiggling off the table since all of them are going off at the same time." Keeping those lines open is the way women get some peace of mind.

Because women, and especially moms, are the central connectors, what happens when cell phone companies refuse to let customers keep their phone numbers when they switch carriers? According to a recent news story, this is the policy of most service providers. Specifically, it is a marketing ploy to retain customers and make switching difficult. That phone number is her lifeline to her kids, their school, her job, her parents, the doctor—you name it. For that reason alone, many customers will not switch, choosing security over savings and services.

This marketing strategy is an example of the pitfall of designing retention programs that may have short-term revenue gains at the expense of women's longer-term loyalty and trust. Another issue that many marketers may not have taken into account is that women, who are often the ones to wrestle with customer service issues related to home and family, now handle those calls on the run (using cell phones instead of landlines). Longer waiting times and complicated dial-around runarounds on automated service numbers become more exasperating to her when the costly cell phone minutes are piling up. What if she takes it out on your brand?

Reach Out and (Try to) Touch Someone

For four years I was CEO of N. W. Ayer & Partners, the first ad agency in the United States. For nearly 90 years, AT&T (formerly the Bell system) was a treasured Ayer client. Now merged with another agency, Ayer was once famous for one of the best new-technology taglines of all time, "Reach Out and Touch Someone." Oddly enough, that line was written nearly 20 years ago to encourage long-distance telephoning, long before the invention of the Internet, PDAs, or voicemail. Yet it still captures the leading benefit of technology, especially for women, because technology is the great enabler that helps them reach out to the people and places of their lives.

One woman told me, "I like the Internet because when I first moved away, I missed home so much, and I was on the phone all the time. Now I use the Internet." Another boasted, "I send my sister digital pictures of my nieces so she is able to watch them grow up." A third woman said, "I am on the computer all day at work. And I communicate with my family. I communicate with my kid's school. I've gotten my mother to use it. We can't wait to get on together every day."

Alternatively, women also see the downside of too much connection, especially as it relates to their children. One woman complained, "I have nephews who, instead of playing sports, are on the computer as many hours as God will give." Another said, "I tell my daughter sometimes you have to go outside, just to look at the sky. And I don't care what kind of graphics you have, it's just not the same as looking at that big autumn moon." One woman likened her computer to an additional family member: "I think technology is like a mother-in-law because it can be good and bad. And it can really take up your time."

Conversely, the computer can rob women of live intimacy. One woman put it this way: "If you sit down and you're writing a letter, the thoughts just kind of flow—versus when you're online, you might get bumped, someone calls you, the telephone rings. I think writing on the computer is less from the heart."

It is interesting that Ayer also created a TV campaign for AT&T called You Will. In the You Will commercials, written in the mid-1990s, consumers were promised that one day they could send a fax from the water's edge at the beach, take a course in a classroom on the other side of the world from home, and drive through a highway toll booth without stopping to pay. Of course, wireless laptops, long-distance learning, and E-ZPass all came true, even sooner than expected. My favorite commercial in the campaign showed a mom in an airport, kissing her baby at home goodnight by cooing to it on a videophone. That is intimacy, but why has it not become more widespread? Sure beats faxing from the beach for most working moms who have to travel. Is technology fully delivering on women's desires to reach out?

As I discussed in Chapter 4, women are masters of the full range of receiving communication from others. They interpret eye contact, facial expressions, body language, and tone of voice. Technology cheats those stimuli. Men thrive in the single path of contact that technology affords them. Joan Meyers-Levy, associate marketing professor at the University of Chicago, has observed in her studies that "men eliminate and women integrate when processing information." She says that "women appear to have more connections between the right and left hemispheres of the brain and they may use both sides actively when processing information. With more connections between the hemispheres, women may be better able to do a variety of tasks simultaneously that draw on the powers of both sides."[8]

That is why connections are the real benefit of technology for women. It is no surprise that e-mail and instant messaging are favorite Internet features for women. Nearly 60 percent of women online say that they receive at least 11 e-mails per day (versus 49 percent of men).[9] Seen through a woman's stress filter, e-mail is the surrogate for the phone call and the quick way to write a letter, and it secretly helps assuage the guilt of not staying in closer touch. The now-famous intonation of "You've got mail" is the cyber equivalent of "You are wanted or remembered by someone." Instant messaging, adopted especially by young girls who send and receive dozens each day, takes "I love you" to "I love you now," even if the content of the message is simply "ditto."

Broadband providers tout the quick downloading of images and the reduction of waiting time. One of the unsung benefits of high-speed access is that women can get in touch faster, have peace of mind sooner, and know that their life needs are within reach in an instant. Marketers who focus on the benefit of speedier connections are playing into what women really want.

A Kiss Is Still a Kiss

Even with its assets, technology can come up short for women. A woman in one of my sessions described it this way: "The Internet's great, technology's great, computers are great. But it does take away from me talking to you. It takes away from me understanding you. Because everything is black and white on the Internet. You don't get to relate." Another woman explained, "I can send a nasty e-mail to you because I don't like the way you responded to me. Well, I don't know what your heart felt. If I had been talking to you, I might have realized, 'Man, she's had a bad day,' and I'd say, 'Hey, are you okay?'"

Just like the boyfriend mentioned in the quote at the beginning of this chapter (imagine proposing on voicemail!), some corporations don't get women. Women hear and respond to the emotional undertones of electronic and telephonic communication. Why does this matter to you as a marketer? Successful marketers work to imbue their brands with a personality so that women have both a rational and an emotional reason to choose them over competitors. Does the technology strategy of your marketing plan include this kind of insight? Do you design personal connections into your software? Does your website or phone bank look and feel like your brand? Remember how much women are attuned to details. They can see and feel the disconnects.

As I said earlier, most decisions for women are not "just business" or "just peanut butter" or "just a car"; they are personal. Your brand communications, live or technically enhanced, should reflect that truth. However, what happens when, as a marketer, you do not have face-to-face contact and your store or service counter is purely virtual—online or on the phone? When women are on your site, they cannot hear your voice. When they shop from your online business, they cannot see your salesperson's face (thanks to the retail ills of Chapter 4, that is the reason women retreat to online shopping). How about the ubiquitous automated customer service line? How is that working for women?

Smooth Operator

When a woman calls your customer service line and gets your automated answering system, she can usually hear nothing but the sound of her own screams of frustration because the abuses of this invention may have resulted in the worst way to connect with women about your brand. To her, it's press "M" for murder: "Automated voicemail bugs me. I can't stand it. It's like road rage. I want real people to give me real answers. No voicemail."

Even systems that are automated to direct callers through the maze of company departments can backfire: "I hate it when people who work in different departments have no idea what people who work in other departments do. Like if you call and you actually press 2 and you tell them your problem, and they say, 'Okay, that's not us. Let me transfer you.' And you get transferred 50 million times. It really makes me angry." Another woman complained, "How about people who don't know what they're doing when they answer the phone, or people who don't like their 'phone jobs' who answer, 'Hello' with a bad attitude?"

As a marketer, when you use technology to facilitate your customer service with women, realize that they have expectations of service and courtesy that are equal across all elements of your communications. Just because your customer line is conveniently open 24 hours does not mean that your operators may be rude. Lands' End has a tremendous reputation for humanizing its customer service line. The brand that invented the flattering Kindest Cut swimsuit for women put that same personal care into its hiring and training of telephone order representatives. That same ease of use translated onto their Internet site, which has features such as a live chat room where an instant messaging system allows you to interact with a friendly and speedy advisor. Just by logging on, you can ask for gift suggestions for your tall, conservative sister, and the advisor will send back ideas, photos to look at, and sizing and color information—just like her counterpart on the phone. The next challenge for Lands' End is to maintain that same quality of connection with women when representatives are face to face with them in the apparel departments of their new partner, Sears.

Lesson 2. Humanize Your Technology

Automated systems are often cost-saving measures. Phone trees can save time by directing incoming calls to the appropriate departments. How can marketers create systems that are efficient but let customers detour around the voicemail maze? Some women would rather communicate through an anonymous message center, but for the many who do not, why not make the first button-press option enable callers to connect to a human being? Some companies have purposefully put the human option at step 8 or 9 to avoid human contact at all costs. Beware: It will cost you eventually. Besides, I have recently heard women tell their friends how to anticipate and avoid the phone tree scams: "Push zero, the pound key, or the star key, anything but what they tell you." A woman telling a woman is a more effective and trusted communication process than your recorded "Please press" message.

Marketer Martha Stewart, whose multichannel business depends on her expertise and precise style, records her own voice as the greeting when you call her mail-order company, Martha by Mail. When you dial, you can hear Martha's smooth but determined voice welcoming you and promising that she will monitor all calls for quality service. However, be careful what you promise if you humanize your system. I ordered a special kitchen trash can in "Martha's green" (see how far women will go to get the details right?), and it did not arrive. I called three or four times, each time getting a new promise that it would arrive in just a couple of days. After two months of waiting, I called again and told the customer service representative, "Look, Martha said that she was monitoring this call for quality, so I want something done." Fear of Martha got results. (Now, however, Martha's experiences in the financial sector will likely lessen her company's reliance on the humanization of a single brand guardian.)

As custodian of your brand, can you create human connections by integrating your website and your customer service line? That way, a customer can leave you a voice message, and then you can instant message your response to her within minutes for questions like, "Is this true to size?" "Does the bag match the shoes?" and "What does the gift wrap look like?" Redenvelope.com has live chat rooms where the customer service people are always available for questions. This enables the company to insert some intimacy into an automated world. E-mail reminder options, assuming they are an opt-in feature, are a great support for busy women, whether for buying Dad's birthday gift or scheduling mammograms.

Delta Airlines e-mails subscribers to Delta Deals updates on low-cost, last-minute getaway flights. 1800Flowers.com e-mails customers to let them know that a birthday or holiday is coming up with a reminder of what was sent last year to help the gift giver remember well-received or favorite flowers. Both of these companies understand that women have good intentions but are often too busy to plan ahead and need the support.

Love the One You're With

As long as the hold is not too long, women can tolerate the computer voices at 800 numbers, especially if the voices have a little bit of personality and a sense of humor. Women's apparel company Title IX Sports uses a recording of a woman with a local accent who pops on as you are waiting to encourage you to hang in there. American Airlines provides a recorded way to check on flight departures and arrivals and uses an extremely friendly female voice that says colloquial things like, "Don't worry; I'll figure it out." If your relationships have to be automated, at least let your robot be creative and responsive in the ways an expert service person would be. Humanize the technology as much as you can.

Just Ask Jim McCann, Chairman and CEO of 1800Flowers.com . . .

It is easier to add humanity to computerized systems if you understand the essence of your brand: "Whether we admit it or not, we all strive for social intimacy. Nothing makes you feel better than to love and be loved. The nice thing about our business is that we foster other people's ability to express themselves. Because of the Internet, because of the convenient access channels, the telephone, the PDAs, our job is to use technologies that are cold and impersonal to make our experience, both with our customers and with the people in their lives, more personal. Women have thoughtful ideas all day long. Your niece is going back to school, and you want to do something about it. Your cousin has a birthday, and she lives in Philadelphia. You think these thoughts in the shower, working out, waiting for the bus. Our technologies are meant to be so convenient that you act on a higher percentage of those thoughtful intentions you already have, which will make your life richer and makes people more appreciative of you, more connected to you. Isn't that a wonderful business to be in?"

Even though Jim's business started as brick and mortar flower shops and then grew through its eponymous 800 number, most women trusted the brand enough to shift their usage to online ordering, which now accounts for more than half of the company's revenue. However, some categories require a little more of the human handholding afforded them by the live customer-service telephone line, and some of them have figured out how to make the customer service line work as both a brand supporter and a customer connection. A generous helping of skilled human beings who know how to listen is generally included.

> ### Just Ask Rob Matteucci, President of Color and Professional Coloring at Clairol, Inc. . . .
>
> *Rob Matteucci is president of the worldwide Clairol hair-coloring and professional coloring division of Procter & Gamble. If there were ever a category that came with the emotional risk and need for immediate support and education, it is home hair coloring. And Clairol was a pioneer in getting it right. Rob describes it this way: "First, the best education is person to person. That could be her mom, her sister, and her stylist. I think that women want to talk about hair coloring. Not be talked at, but talk about it. I could go and have a conversation with every woman in the salon, and we would be better off, so as close to that as possible is what we aim for. The next best thing [to being in person] is the 800 line because you have a confidant. We probably have the best 800 lines in the business because the people who work on those lines, especially the ones in New York, have been there for years. The number of minutes we spend on the phone is far longer than any other company in the business by a long run. It's next best because it's a conversation. They are playing minishrink. We try to minimize time on hold, and we have a very disciplined follow-up system. If we think we missed a consumer call, we go back. We take it very seriously. Are we perfect? No. But I think we are the best at being responsive and available." Rob's strategy continues to focus on the seamless connection between the brand and its voice, as keys to helping women understand the product at the moment of decision at the shelf, as well as at the moment of truth in the mirror.*

Technology can be the bridge that recognizes that women are utilizing more than one channel to find and buy your brand. The retail shopper gets tired of the vigilante process in the store and becomes a catalog or 800 shopper. The online browser decides to pick up the phone to order once she has had the private time to search the brand's website. A recent phenomenon is that the online shopper has started to go to the store to pick up merchandise to avoid the high shipping costs and narrow windows for delivery times. Who is the one who has to wait at home for the UPS guy? Ask a woman, and she will tell you more often than not that it is she. Thus she makes the channels work *her* way.

This interchannel behavior was supported by research that Just Ask a Woman conducted in May 2002 with Burst! Media, a consortium of websites that see traffic from a large number of women. Nearly 4,000 women weighed in on questions related to the role of the Internet in the shopping experience, with answers like these: Two thirds of the women polled said that they use the Internet to browse, research, and compare products. For a majority of these women (nearly 68 percent), the Internet is their primary information source about products and services, ranging from 49 percent of women in the 55- to 64-year-old group to a high of 62.5 percent of the women who were 25 to 34.[10]

Although the majority of these women browsed, researched, and compared products online, four in ten will still purchase offline, and only one in ten said that she nearly always purchases online. Marketers ought to think of their website as their store window or their virtual aisles for shoppers to see, decide, and compare. Keep them free of clutter and pop-up interruptions, and have virtual salespeople on call if questions need answering. In 2002, both ivillage.com and AOL decided to eliminate most pop-up ads from their sites. Do not complicate your site with too many features. She is there only if you make it simple.

Tom Holliday, president of the Retail Advertising and Marketing Association, told me that he attributes women's predilection for preshopping online to the time pressures that women face. "There is a certain level of impersonal service delivered by technology, where the expectations are lower, but in some cases the delivery is higher. For example, on Amazon.com, women are finding out that they can shop in many channels at the same time (like

Target and Toys R Us), so that when they go to a store, the decision is pretty much made. Or if they research on the Internet, they can easily go to the catalog to buy. Women are smarter in using all those permutations."

Lesson 3. Integrate Your Channels by Integrating Your Technology

Women are comfortable with moving back and forth among their options, which renders earlier marketer's fears that their websites would hurt their in-store business moot. Each feeds the other. Is your online site as professional and customer-oriented as is your in-store experience? Remember, with a click of her mouse, a woman can be on to the next storefront, with the same prices, if you do not make her first encounter worthwhile. By the way, if your brand has no Web presence as late as 2002, you should know that many women might question your legitimacy as a modern marketer.

Just Ask Tina Johnson, CEO of Saks Fifth Avenue . . .

Tina Johnson has designed the integration of her channel communications from the perspective of her customers' needs. With its long history as a designer emporium, Saks has broadened its reach by extending its store online, by catalog, and in person. Tina explains, "I think the most important thing is to realize that the needs of female customers are quite varied. It is not a one-stop shop. There are many types of women, and they have different needs in terms of how you attend to them, and how you speak to them, and really how you connect with them, which I think is most important. Whether it is the catalog or the Internet, the

(continued)

(Continued)

female consumer uses them dually, and they have become tremendous research vehicles for her. It not only allows her to buy direct, but it allows her to be educated as to what the fashion trends are for that particular season, what designer looks may be important for them. Then they come into the store to be serviced. It is still a very demanding service environment for time-pressed people. In fall of 2002, we were the first, right from the runway, to be able to directly e-mail those shots to our customers right off the runway. So, if we attend a Prada show, within 48 hours, those shots will be e-mailed to our customers who wear Prada. Our database comes from our own sales associates, so we know who to send them to, based on their relationship with the company." Tina's plan not only integrated her channels for women but also respected the consumer's needs for control because the runway program was initiated through existing, validated relationships with personal sales associates.

I have my own example of triumphing through an intertwining Internet/phone/store shopping experience. I was on a business trip in April and detoured through a mall (OK, it was attached to the hotel) and walked into a Restoration Hardware store. There I saw the most wonderful metal glider for my front porch in Pennsylvania. It was that retro 1940s kind of rocker that my grandparents would have swung back and forth on. It went instantly onto my mental must-buy list. Because I was in another city, though, I was unable to do anything about it. I returned home and forgot about it until I received a Restoration Hardware catalog in the mail. There it was again. Then I thought I would go online to see if they had it in another color. I saw it in butter yellow, clicked on it, and ordered. However, when the weather warmed up and I still had no glider, I turned to the phone. The people at their 800 number told me it would not arrive until late June. A porch glider that misses Memorial Day, no way! I hung up and called the Restoration Hardware store in my Manhattan neighborhood. They had the glider in stock. It would be heavy and difficult to transport, but at least I would have it. After all that effort, I canceled the online order, picked up the glider from the store, and happily rocked my way through May and June.

Was the delay frustrating? Yes. However, I felt such entrepreneurial pride that I had used all their kinds of stores to get what I wanted. Now, if only they had pointed out the timing options to me at the start. Why did I have to integrate their channels for them?

Looking for Love in All the Wrong Places

What is amazing about the infiltration of online activity among women is that it has now penetrated every area of their lives. Women talk about Googling prospective blind dates to see if they are a good catch. While women are able to name search engines such as Yahoo.com, they are not loyal to too many websites or portals, as was the intent of so many dot-coms gone by. Instead, they type in the words they want to learn about, whether 401Ks or "ache in side." Women are researching online for financial counsel, health diagnoses, decorating ideas, and even trivia. As one woman said, "We were having drinks at my house, and for some stupid reason my husband and I started arguing about how old Regis Philbin is, so I jumped on the computer and proved I was right."

Lots of their usage is more serious: "I do a lot of research online because there are hundreds of sites out there. I have probably diagnosed myself 50 times." Note that this woman never claimed that her diagnoses were correct, just that it gave her an answer. Marketers should realize that women derive tremendous satisfaction and confidence when they have their opinions validated, even if it is by a website. That may even account for the prevalence of online polls, where once you cast your vote, you can see how others voted to confirm just how right you were.

Online research can also be liberating and fun for women. Prior to the stock market troubles of 2002, one woman told me, "I'm just starting to get into trading myself. I used to have all my money in a major brokerage house. My girlfriend said, 'Are you crazy? You can do this all on your own.' I'm always on the Internet. So I think I'm just going to get into it and have some fun, so I can watch and trade by myself."

Online research is also transforming female auto shoppers: "I get all the information I possibly can about the value, get it narrowed down, and then I will call the dealer and tell them, 'When you can get me this car for this price, then I'll come in to buy it.' I like to go in there and be the person with the knowledge and the power."

She Gets to Be the One to Say "I Do"

This online communication, whether for shopping or researching, has come with a penalty. Women are learning that their personal information is not always guarded, and the resultant invasion of uninvited sales pitches, spam, and pornography makes them wary and angry. Her own online experience is only one of her concerns. First of all, she is usually the last one to get online in a given day. Her kids and her husband all get dibs before she does. Women are incredibly concerned about the effect that privacy-invading Internet interlopers have on their families, particularly their children: "I wonder how you can keep your kids from clicking on it all," wondered one woman. Another asked, "What protections are provided so that my 11-year-old son doesn't get us tickets to Disney World?"

Beyond the quick weight loss and Viagra pitches and the "you must read this" spam, e-mail boxes are also victims of assaults by legitimate marketers. A recent incident in pharmaceutical marketing drew consumer criticism and government action. Certain drugstores decided to convert their customer database of information about drug usage and conditions into a direct-mail effort for a derivative formula of the drug Prozac. Consumers were angry that their personal information was ammunition for sampling new drugs. How many people know I am depressed? What else are you going to sell to me just because I buy from you? This kind of betrayal of trust leads to further suspicion, especially among women. Stores like Eckerd quickly stated that they would give out information only with a customer's written and validated permission.

Women's reluctance to be marketed to without their consent is an issue that I have heard about many times: "It's Big Brother watching. They know exactly what I'm interested in. It makes me feel uncomfortable. When I call the cable company, it is amazing to me how our conversation goes. It's like they can see where I am in the house and what I'm doing. They know that much about me." Another woman worried about the aftermath of saying yes to an interactive pitch: "Is there going to be some kind of protection? If I send away for a brochure, are they going to sell my information and then suddenly at 9 P.M., I'm getting all kinds of phone calls? Now they know I like country music. More phone calls and junk mail."

Lesson 4. Consent Marketing Means She Opts In and She Opts Out

Think of it as a "Mother, may I?" strategy. When women see sales pitches coming into their living rooms via TV, their computers via e-mail, and their phones via telemarketers, they beg me to tell marketers to give them choice. *Consent marketing* means inviting a woman to tell you when you are allowed to sell to her and talk to her. Unsolicited e-mail reminders and pop-up ads that obscure programming are the kind of technology strategies that make her cringe. Realize that when women are watching TV, searching online, or just enjoying a friend's phone call, your intrusion is not welcome. Even her complaints are being channeled into more sales ploys.

Lately, companies are training their customer service people to pitch new products when the consumer calls. For some companies, the short-term results are worth the risk of ticking customers off. According to a July 2002 article in the *Wall Street Journal*, companies from Verizon to Wells Fargo are experimenting with this: "More than 3,000 phone reps at Citigroup are dabbling in sales [so that] last year, Citigroup's call-center staff sold 4.3 million products to current customers—six times as many as two years ago." But the article carries this warning from Kathleen Peterson of Powerhouse Consulting: "How will you sell something to someone who's calling up because they've just found their fifteenth billing error?"[11] Keep that up and get ready to meet the virtual vigilante shopper.

Will You Still Love Me Tomorrow?

We interviewed 100 women about some of the technologies emerging on the horizon, called *convergence* by the cognoscenti. Women see it as the Jetsons come to life. Women are realists. They know that Star Wars technology is coming to their living rooms whether they like it or not. Ordering products from a television screen, typing e-mails to friends during favorite shows, tuning into the TV-turned-computer for a personal traffic report on your own commute—all these seem possible, but not all are desirable. Women's worries are practical ones: If I order something from the TV, do I pay the cable company for it? Will they take my sweater back if it does not fit? Are their credit terms as good as Visa's?

Talking with women about current and emerging technologies can get pretty emotional. Women recognize that the way they communicate and the way that companies communicate with them affect the quality of their lives, as well as their families' lives. The growing pile of remote controls that multiply like rabbits puzzles her. She dreads a computer in every room, as well as the idea that she will snuggle into bed with one at night. As one woman said, "I want my computer in a separate room and my TV in a separate room. I don't have to be near the computer if I don't want to be. That's my quiet time. I don't have much of that with two small kids." (Her desperate need for quiet time is the subject of Chapter 8.)

Some major marketers are still just coming to grips with the influence of women on emerging and converging technologies. I spoke about women and convergence at a panel on broadband segmentation at the Cable Television Advertising and Marketing Conference in January 2002. Before I went onstage, one of the major research experts started her speech by acknowledging that the most influential group to watch would be women. Although that was true, it surprised me that she presented it as new news. Who else controls the TV set and computer usage in the house? Who else tries to converge opinions when Cindy wants to watch the PowerPuff Girls and Stan wants to watch the Ryder Cup finals? Who's buying most of what comes into the house, online or off? It's the lady of the house. She is the one who invented convergence, even if she calls it multitasking. Listen to her and know when to leave her alone.

Lesson 5. Learn the Differences among Off-Line, Online, and Out of Line

Although women appreciate the virtues of technology and connection, they need time to chill out. Just because you can sell it does not mean that she needs or wants it. As difficult as it is to stop adding one more sales pitch to your service lines, one more pop-up to your programming, or one more clever way to begin a tele-marketing call, try to discipline this part of your outreach strategy. **Ask yourself, "Would I want my mom interrupted with this call? Would I want my wife or sister to see this banner ad recurring when she's e-mailing a friend?" If your answers are no, then why invade the privacy of your female customers? They need a break.** And taking a break is something they like to do with other humans, not with your virtual sales force.

In an idealized media-filled world, the Internet and converged television and computers would create a seamless community where women can interact and intersect. Community is probably the most overused and underdelivered concept in female sites—and I don't hear women begging for community with strangers. They're looking for information more than intimacy.

Most women I talk to are purposeful in their online activity. They go online when they want to find something out, they want to buy something, or they want to play. If they want to talk, though, they would kill for a half hour with their real-world girlfriends or moms. Whether the time is spent laughing over drinks, talking on the phone, or instant messaging each other, that is the community that women really seek. Exceptions to this rule include shows like Liz Dolan's "Satellite Sisters," which involves real, live women who are easy to relate to. Other online successes include chat rooms and bulletin boards about health conditions and parenting, such as those on ivillage.com. WeightWatchers.com has one of the most active bulletin boards I have ever seen. The members talk about everything from what to buy at Trader Joe's to good restaurants with healthy food, or members can choose to talk to other women who have the same amount of weight to lose.

The message boards that attract interest are the ones that are specific, information-filled, and emotionally gratifying. Another great example is a wedding site called theknot.com. Brides bond over wedding planning and share secrets beyond flower arrangements, such as advice about mothers-in-law. In addition, some websites can give marketers a look at what consumers think of them. Planetfeedback.com encourages customers to talk about examples of a company's good or bad customer service. Are you monitoring what women are saying on there? Have you looked at your brand reviews on epinions.com? It is like uncovering the word on the street online.

While in Chapter 3 I described a woman's board of directors as a group of living, trusted advisors, your technology-enhanced marketing can either earn you a cyberseat on that board or get your brand voted off. Similar to a new romantic relationship, women are keenly attuned to the details and nuances regarding how you use technology to speak to her. A woman may be on the brink of falling in love—but only if you fall in line.

Cracking the Code on Intimacy with Technology

1. *The best technological advancement is the one that eases her life.* It is tempting to apply the latest, greatest, new thing—not only to electronic product introductions but also to your systems and software. Start first, though, by asking women how they use or need what you are inventing. She may save you money by simplifying it—and reward you with her dollars for listening.

2. *Humanize your technology.* Women observe and experience communication nuances even when they are digital. Weaving the language and intuitive usage of human emotion into your technology strategy will separate you from your competition and enhance your brand value.

3. *Integrate your channels by integrating your technology.* Creating complementary channels for your product is only half the job. Linking them in practical, real-world ways for women is another. Improving your website does not hurt your store; it is like dressing your store window to invite more women inside.

4. *Consent marketing means she opts in and she opts out.* Women crave and demand choice. As much as you might like to trap them into your commercial lair, they will find a way out. Women protect their families and their privacy. Sounds obvious, but they matter more to women than does your sales pitch.

5. *Learn the differences among off-line, online, and out of line.* Back to the stress filter of Chapter 2, realize that women's lives include you more and more each day, thanks to technology. Women welcome the fluid way that they can access you anytime, anywhere. But sometimes women need to shut down. Do not overstay your welcome.

Throughout this chapter I have reminded you of how often women put the needs of others before their own. Just how far does that go? As a marketer, how can you make her first in your world if she is last in her own? The next chapter gives you the tools.

CHAPTER 7

Demanding Respect

You're just another ring on the register.

"R-E-S-P-E-C-T, find out what it means to me," as the old song goes. There is no better way to capture women's expectations for how they want to be treated by people who want their business. (Imagine them belting it out like Aretha Franklin, and you've got their tone of voice, too.) You may be thinking, "Whoa, both men and women want respect, and they both deserve it." True. But having interviewed thousands of women, I've learned that women do not feel respected as customers. Many see differences in the way men and women are treated in similar circumstances. Unfortunately, you are not the only one who is putting women at the end of the line. They feel that their families sometimes do it, too. Surprisingly, they even do it themselves.

A woman I interviewed put it this way: "In our society, women don't get the respect that men do. A lot of women aren't even aware of it because we're almost trained to look past it and not even recognize it." This chapter looks deeply into why and how this happens and into how you, as a marketer, can win with women by showing them the respect that they covet.

In the last chapter I talked about how to communicate with women online without getting out of line. However intimate, your website and 800 numbers still keep you at arm's length from her. Although you can build humanity into your digital and telephone communications, at some point your business comes face to face with women, particularly if you are in the service provider sector, such as the medical community, financial advising, hotel and travel industries, and other personal businesses that rely on relationships.

Either respect is written on your face, your policies, and your language, or it is not. Women, with their ability to observe you with all senses blazing, are amazing lie detectors, so your respect has to be genuine. This chapter spells out the ways that women demand respectful relationships from various categories in which personal service is a critical piece of closing the sale. This chapter reveals just how disrespectful some customer relationships have become and offers ideas on how you can guide your business to a daily code of productive behavior with women. You will learn how to anticipate a woman's feelings and needs so that you can speak woman to her.

When women give you the precious gift of their time, they expect your respect and attention in return. For example, led by their frustration with the health care industry (since health is the most pressing issue in many women's lives), many women are unhappy with the lack of listening they receive from the people who want their dollars and loyalty. Instead of feeling that, as the customer, they come first, many women say that they feel last in your line.

I interviewed an executive in the fashion industry who told me something that first seemed harsh but then, I have to admit, true. I asked him why some women felt intimidated by luxury stores and their designers. He told me that the problem rests with the women themselves: "If they don't have confidence, they walk into our stores with a chip on their shoulders, expecting to be ignored. So, when the least little slight occurs, these women are vindicated in a 'See, I told you so' sort of way. Confident women don't perceive slights as disrespect. And they don't bring it on, either."

My first reaction to this executive was that he was shirking responsibility for the behavior of his salespeople. But the more I listened to women talk about their presumed status in relationship situations, the more I was able to see some of the truth in what he said. Many women put themselves last in line, even behind the occasional sales staffers who sometimes intimidate them.

Last in Line

Why does she feel last in the first place? My feeling is that women do it to themselves out of a sense that I call *otherness*. During much of my research I found that in a woman's hierarchy of devoting her time, care, and energy, others' needs come first in so many aspects of her life.

This otherness is in stark contrast to the messages put forward particularly in women's magazines, where the "me first" focus has outlasted the Me Generation of the 1970s. As I discussed in Chapter 5, the mantra of self-esteem has encouraged women to take time out to care for themselves and explore their personal, as well as professional, potentials. Thus I was somewhat surprised to see that while women crave time for themselves, they still willingly and lovingly devote it to others.

Many women defer to family first, but friends, colleagues, bosses, neighbors, and even strangers in a checkout line also get their time. It may not seem like a big deal if women put themselves last when shopping for designer apparel or buying groceries. However, this behavior is more frightening when it is literally a matter of life and death. In one of our sessions, a very mild-mannered woman kept making subtle points about how women need to be strong and take care of their own health.

Suddenly, near the end of session, as she listened to some of the younger women describe how they postponed going to the doctor or consumed only Diet Cokes and Snickers candy bars, she cleared her throat and silenced the room with this story: "I knew that I had been having stomach pains for a number of years. But I kept putting off going to the doctor. There were so many other things going on with my family at the time. When I finally went to check it out, I learned I had stomach cancer. I am in remission now, but I am warning you to start thinking about yourselves before it's too late." As stunning as this revelation was, I have heard numerous similar stories over the years. Diseases undiagnosed. Miscarriages that could have been prevented. Women letting their own needs slide because of their kids, their jobs, the money. Believe me, if she feels like she is last in line, it's because she is.

Counting Worries, Not Sheep

Her last-in-line status is not confined to the daylight hours. Concerns about her family keep her up at night. Many women lay awake with their mental to-do lists scrolling through their heads, thinking about the day before and the day to come. I have asked women how they fall asleep, especially compared to how their husbands do. It seems that he snores while she lies awake worrying. As one woman said to her husband, "Gosh, it took me an hour to fall asleep last night. I was thinking about our bills and the kids. And he answered, 'Not me. Boy, I was asleep as soon as my head hit the pillow.'" The result, naturally, is that she is tired when she starts the "real day" again.

It Is Her Job to Be Last

Women's rationale for being so other-focused is tied to the language of *duty*: "I'm not allowed to have a time-out." I am a case in point. I know that I always bragged about earning perfect attendance awards in school. No faux tummy aches. No hiding under the covers to avoid a test. My perfect record was a signal that no one had to worry about me. As I grew up and moved into my career, I kept that no-sick-days mentality, still earning that attendance certificate to prove that I was responsible and self-sufficient rather than needy. Honestly, I wonder if I had not simply bought into the super-careerist myth that I was just too busy (or important) to allow myself a sick day or a missed meeting.

At home, women allow both children and husbands to get ahead of them in line. One woman told me, "My kids are spoiled. If I don't cook three or four side dishes with the meat, they say, 'Is that all you made?' So I cook a lot. There is always the push for me to do more, 'I want French Toast. No, I want an omelet. I want gravy.'"

While there are lots of helpful husbands out there, I have heard many women say that sometimes husbands add to their duties. As one woman said, "It's not uncommon for my husband to call on Friday and say, 'I've invited a family of five over for dinner,' so I need to keep a lot of stuff in the freezer." Another woman confided, "My husband says, 'Please don't ever give me a TV dinner,' so one of the first meals I ever fixed was a TV dinner. Before he got home, I put it on a plate and heated it up in the microwave, and he never knew."

Be careful when you try to make your brand a salve for otherness. A recent commercial for the Friendly's restaurant chain told the story of a husband who takes a day off from work to enjoy his children. In the voiceover, he notes that while he is home playing with the kids for just one weekday, his wife (who looks happy but weary with housework) is there every day. So, he treats them all to a meal at Friendly's to make up for it. The wife is pictured as gratefully glowing. I wonder how a woman would see the fairness in balancing her 365 days of hard work with a Friendly's lunch. The commercial risks coming off as comical rather than respectful. Tell the story from a woman's point of view, and your chances of getting it right increase.

An example of that technique is a recent commercial for Jif peanut butter. In the spot, the mom is at the table doing homework, which is actually hers because she is going back to school. Her little boy watches her and asks if he can help. She says no in an appreciative way. He heads to the kitchen and makes her a peanut butter sandwich. Her reaction to his empathy and sweetness is priceless. That is respect on her terms.

Lesson 1. Move Her from Last in Her Line to First in Yours

This is as simple as looking at the way you address her—as herself, not as Jane's mom or Mrs. So-and-So. How are your business hours scheduled? Do they accommodate a working mom's life or your own needs? If you are an apparel retailer, do you tailor her clothes for free or just his? If a man walks into your dealership at the same time as a woman with kids, whose hand do you shake first? Does your salesperson hustle to greet the single woman?

Her List of Others Goes On and On

Women's concerns about others do not stop with their husbands and children. Many are responsible for their own parents and in-laws. One woman named Margaret described her full-time day job at the office and her full-time night job caring for her aging mother who lived with her: "You tell yourself, 'Margaret, get a grip. Just get the job done.'"

Ironically, one of the best ways to motivate women to take care of themselves is to acknowledge their responsibility to others: "As a mother, it's your responsibility to make sure you're healthy." Certainly health insurance companies have milked the claim of being there for them because women are so other-motivated.

I know many women who assume the helpful job role even when they are the customers. I know women who will hang up clothes that have fallen off the sale rack. Others carefully place a grocery item back on the exact shelf it came from when they change their minds about buying it. This happens even at the higher-priced customer venues, such as airlines. I have noticed that in first class, the flight attendants help the male passenger pull out his tray table and gently unfold the tablecloth onto it. I whip my tray table out on my own, and take the tablecloth from the attendant, and unfold it myself. I notice that women clean up their seat area. Women help. If I travel in a navy blue suit, other passengers often ask me, "When does this flight get in?" (It's that "How may I help you?" look, I guess.)

This behavior of being last in line exhibits itself in all kinds of circumstances. At the end of business meetings in conference rooms, I have seen female attendees pick up the coffee cups and wipe the table. I have done it myself many times. When I see people just walk out and leave a mess, I wonder, "Do you think your mother works here?" which is scary because that just feeds the last-in-line syndrome.

Why do a woman's feelings of being last in line matter to you as a marketer or service provider? By the time a woman comes face to face with your brand, your store, your message, or your people, she has shelved many of her own needs for others. Now, it is her turn to be first. Do you treat her that way? Do your services make her feel truly first-class, or, like her family or employer, are you implying by your attitude and policies that she should get in line?

Discover Card ran a commercial recognizing that women crave that first-in-line status. The spot tells the story of a mother whose growing boys are eating her out of house and home. She is the one charged with buying so many groceries to supply them. By using the

Discover Card, she can get cash back for herself, exemplified by the scene of her standing in the grocery checkout line looking at a travel magazine with a cover shot of a deserted beach. That is marketing to her underlying desire to be first once in a while.

Remember, She's the One with the Wallet

Lisa Caputo, president of the Women & Co. division of Citigroup, noted the predisposition of financial services companies to focus attention on men: "My perception is that they have never really taken women seriously as an economic power, as investors. When you get statements from various brokerage houses, if you have an account, your husband has an account, and your kids have an account, that statement goes to the male head of household. There was never recognition that women are the earners and contributors to the overall economic well-being of our economy. Couple that with the fact that they outlive men and that the average age of widowhood is 56." One woman explained, "Respect is important. Don't say, 'Do you think you need to discuss this with your husband?' There is none. It's up to me." It is her turn to be first.

If this description of women's need for respect seems too personal for you as a marketer, then perhaps the better motivator for change is remembering what her respect means to you. She earns $1 trillion annually.[1] Fifty-eight percent of working women own stocks and bonds. Women make 80 percent of all health care choices.[2] They purchase 65 percent of all new cars. They make up 50 percent of all travelers, an average of 7.9 business trips in the months prior to March 2000.[3] Consider the business benefits of this number-one customer. Following are two marketers who saw the value of respecting women and made it pay out on the bottom line.

Carole Black, president of Lifetime Television, has reaped the benefits of putting women first. Lifetime was the number-one cable network throughout 2001 and 2002. Carole explains, "The reason we are number one is very simple. We make women number one with us. Because women know we care about them, and we are there for them, they have rewarded us in extraordinary ways. The more you do, the more women will tell other women about it. Women are extraordinarily loyal and appreciative when a person, a business, a car does something for them, because they are always doing for others."

Another business that attributes its success to retooling its distribution to serve women is *People* magazine. Ann Moore, chairman and CEO of Time Inc., tells the story of how *People* achieved its worldwide profit leadership status in the magazine industry: "Timing matters. For 20 years, *People* and the various Time Inc. news magazines came out on Monday. And *People* was then the number-one selling magazine in grocery stores in America. But guess what? No women shop in grocery stores on Monday. So, we spent all this time and money racing to market to get you this news, and we put it into the pipeline on a day you are not there. So, a number of years ago, we did an early delivery test, where we put *People* and the news magazines in the grocery stores Friday night. And we got a 15 percent lift in sales. Just from being at the right time. Timing matters to a busy woman. It's a real lesson for all the other products in America that are completely out of sync as to what a real woman's life is like. Cater to my needs when I need it, not when it's convenient for you."

If, as a marketer, you are feeling that this need to ramp up the respect quotient does not apply to your business, the next lesson offers ways that various categories can spell respect.

Lesson 2. Interpret Respect for Your Industry, and Educate Your Employees

Women define respect on different dimensions depending on the financial, emotional, and ego stakes involved. As the apparel executive said earlier, women may have a chip on their shoulders about your business from prior bad experience. A woman may walk into an auto dealership expecting to be ripped off. She may enter a beauty salon thinking that her current style is not pretty enough. She may meet a broker for the first time and assume that she will be pressured. Knowing those hot buttons helps your company understand how to counter that unspoken belief with respectful behavior.

The way a woman defines respect for one business may be different in another. Why? As I described in Chapter 3, women approach your brands and services with their own powerful memories and prejudices. If a woman has been burned by doctors in the past, she is wary of any signals that show her that her new doctor is in a hurry or seems rote in the responses she hears. If she has grown up in a financially conservative household where she was never allowed to make her own money decisions, she will take slight to any indications that she needs an approving signature. Each category comes with its own baggage, yours and hers. What follows is not a prescription for all women in all categories but a sampling of their voices and concerns and the key factors of respect that can make a difference.

Disrespect in Health Care

The health care category encompasses everyone from a woman's personal physician to the pharmacist, the health insurance claims advisor, and all the products and services that she turns to for her own and her family's well-being. To understand her needs in this category, think of how women truly are Dr. Moms. Women who work outside the home, in jobs where their hours are monitored, feel they must sacrifice their own sick days and vacation days for their families' illnesses. If a child is sick, it is more often mom, rather than her husband, who steals time from the job to go to the pediatrician. As a woman said to me, "I have four weeks of vacation. Three of them I used for my kids' doctor appointments. All my sick days are gone for my kids. You lie and call yourself in sick so you can stay home and take care of your kids."

In interviews we conducted for Lifetime Television, 53 percent of women confessed that they are more likely to take their pet to the vet before they would take themselves to the doctors.[4] As one woman simply put it, "We don't take care of ourselves; we take care of everybody else."

A woman also must take care of her husband's health, and that is clear when she describes the differences between the way she handles illness as opposed to the way her husband does. Some women told stories about how well their husbands cared for them when they were sick. The more typical story, however, was that even if a woman is sick, she has to metamorphose into Nurse Nancy for him. A typical story: "As women, if we get sick, we still have to take care of our families. We can't just stop. If the man gets sick, that's it. He's going to bed: 'Honey, will you bring me soup?' I have to keep going and make dinner, no matter how I feel." Another woman indicted her husband's caregiving: "What do I do when I'm sick? I take care of myself. If I admit, 'I'm sick,' my husband says, 'See you later!' and disappears." You should know that as women told me these stories, they were not whining, even though they were annoyed. They were proud. They will be Superwomen, even if it kills them.

Armed with research from the Internet and health journals, these same women are rendered vulnerable when they have to wear a paper hospital gown and sit naked on the metal examining table. They feel angry when they are on the end of a long phone hold with benefits claims analyst, as the minutes of their lunch hours tick away. And since they know too well the role of caregiver, they have high expectations from their health care providers, including health insurance companies, pharmaceutical companies, hospitals, and wellness centers.

In these environments, however, she is treated not like number one, but like a number. One woman told me, "I have left offices where the doctors herd me in like cattle, like I'm a cow." Another said, "I don't feel like a person to them. I am just the number on my insurance card." And a third warned, "I don't want a doctor with his hand on the doorknob."

Women are rudely ignored: "I'll make an appointment and I'll go to the office, and they're not there. They have notes on the door from other patients saying, 'I came to see you at nine, for the appointment you made with me, and you're not here'" or, "The insurance company never calls me back. I have medical problems that need to be resolved."

Probably the complaint that I hear most often from women is that health care professionals do not believe them and dismiss their symptoms: "One doctor walked in while I was keeled over with abdominal pain and said, 'Are you sure this isn't in your head? I think you need to go to a psychiatrist.' I went back later and told him, 'I got a doctor who listened to me. I had surgery, and here's proof that I did not have psychiatric problems.'"

In an interesting study released in the *Journal of the American Medical Association* in 2002, it was revealed that female primary-care doctors spend more time with patients than do male doctors.[5] And they spent the time differently, talking with patients about their lifestyle and emotional issues and involving patients in their care. That is just what some female patients wish all doctors would do. The chairman of the American Medical Association's board of trustees, J. Edward Hill, claimed that the study revealed "what we already know, men and women are a little bit different in their personal style. I don't think it has any bearing on the quality of medicine." The hundreds of women I have interviewed would beg to differ with him.

Because women take their role as Dr. Mom so seriously, the industry has a long way to go to measure up to her high standards. Marketers in these categories can work to improve their bedside manner even if they are connected to her only by phone or web-site. In addition, it is important to recognize her need for response rates that are accelerated in direct proportion to the severity of her customer need. It's not that she is impatient; she has other people who are depending on her.

How Respect Adds Up in Financial Services

When women talk about the financial services category, the sto-ries get personal really fast. So many of women's preconceptions of finance are tied to the way they were raised (to prize or fear money) and to the way they have dealt with money as adults. Women who have lost money due to their parents, a partner's gambling, drugs, or overspending are burned once but never again. They are the Scarlett O'Hara ("I'll never go hungry again") customers.

Women, who have been ignored as earners solely because they are women, may also walk in to a brokerage with a chip on their shoulders: "As I went to sign the contract, he said to me, 'You make a lot of money for a woman.' I walked out." And as one woman said to me, as recently as the year 2002, "The check is al-ways given to the man. Even if I have the charge card, they will still return to the table and give it to him. Truthfully, I am usually the one who makes more money, yet they turn to him." With these insights as a backdrop, it is easy to see why she is on the lookout when she shops for financial advice.

Here are some of her demands for respect in this category:

- *She wants attention when she wants it.* "I want someone who hears what I have to say and gets back to me right away, not when they get around to it."
- *She wants answers from the one she trusts.* "I find it frustrating when I want an answer and the point person always goes to the specialist. There's all this lag time. I'd rather have one person who is skilled, from a time standpoint."

- *She wants experience that is greater than her own.* "The more I see this young lady broker, the less confidence I have in her. I have to do the investigating. She's always looking to me. I'm giving her information."

- *She wants control.* "It's my money; why am I letting someone else make decisions for me? I will take suggestions from my broker, but I feel I should have control. I want to look and delve into it for a while."

Several financial services companies have set up divisions and programs to support women's needs for information and control. The financial firm Neuberger Berman instituted a Women's Partnership, which includes live seminars and a website, that treats high-end female investors as both customers and as women who are curious and intelligent about marketplace and political issues. I have moderated four of these sessions for Neuberger Berman as part of a series on women's leadership, held around the country in conjunction with *Fast Company* magazine. Panelists like Sarah Weddington, who argued Roe versus Wade; Mae Jemison, the first African American female astronaut; and White House reporter Helen Thomas presented their opinions and took questions from potential female investors. Marketers who create an atmosphere of trust and confidence before jumping to the sale have a better chance of getting on women's radar.

Who Is Driving the Car-Buying Decisions?

The automotive industry is fraught with the anxieties of price negotiation, which actually offends many men, too. However, women are the ones who have been on the receiving end of some of the worst treatment. Women have regaled me with by-now familiar stories that range from the dealer who ignores her questions to the one who asks only, "What color are you looking for?" to the endless process of asking the supervisor who must ask another supervisor.

Even the vehicles themselves have a way of branding her for better or for worse. Minivans have been sold to millions of moms who appreciate the value of a roomy, easy-to-drive, easy-to-exit vehicle that can carpool children. In addition, the capacity and size make minivans a home away from home for their never-ending role as chauffeur.

From personal interviews, however, I know that a woman's feelings about the minivan are wrapped up in her sense of identity and self-respect. One woman told me that she has heard minivans called "breeder cars." Many others have told me that minivans are the least sexy cars on the market: "No guy is going to pick you up if he sees you driving a minivan." The most telling comment of all was, "I know I'm a mom; I don't need my car to scream that to the world."

A commercial for the new Honda Odyssey advertises its in-cabin TV with DVD player as a place where moms can hide out and watch while waiting for a routine kid drop-off and pickup. Women loved the spot because it respected their real need for a few minutes of time-out instead of positioning the features as only a way to make kids (others) happy. Does the dealer understand that same sensitivity? Here is what's on women's minds when they shop for cars and trucks:

- *She wants to be respected as an independent woman.* "They just want to know where my husband is."

- *She doesn't want to be played with.* "I hate the game. I've gone in with my chest stuck out, and said, 'This is what I want; you don't have to sell me anything,' but I always feel like my back is up against the wall."

- *She wants respect that is assumed, not earned.* "One of the motivators to buy a luxury car is the treatment you get in customer service. They respect my words, my opinions; they listen to me, and they don't try to take the upper hand or be authoritarian. I feel like I'm in charge."

She sees the brand as evidence of who she is at that point in time. A woman laughed and told me, "I feel younger when I drive a convertible. Guys look at me in that car." (As a convertible driver, I know the feeling!) Another woman said to me, "My car is a perfect reflection of my image." "What do you drive?" I asked. "A Jaguar." The other women smiled. Say no more.

The Ugly Side of Beauty and Fashion

As I described in Chapter 5, a woman carries so many mental images of who she is, should be, and will not be. Is she young enough, thin enough, and fashionable enough to buy this or that? She is very aware of the appearance of the women who work behind beauty counters. She is torn between wanting to be made over and catered to and wanting to be left alone to find her own way.

As she ages, she is even more sensitive to her competition with other women. As one 40-something woman said to me, "I didn't used to notice the younger women on the street with their short skirts and their little shirts. Now, for some reason, they nauseate me." On top of their internal criticism, they even carry the chip of fashionistas past. One woman explained, "Every day, I walk out of the house, and I can still imagine my mother saying, 'You're not going to wear that, are you?'" With all this in her mind, here are some of the demands she has for the beauty and fashion industries.

- *She wants to feel that she is already beautiful.* "As a plus-size woman, I prefer shopping in a regular department where they carry size 16. I don't want to feel as if I'm being lowered by escalator into the elephant bin." On the flip side, a satisfied customer paid this tribute to a store that she frequents: "You walk in, and they give you something to eat and drink. They practically bow down at your feet and say, 'What can I do for you next?'"

- *She wants to be acknowledged.* "After my expensive day of beauty, there was no follow-up. It's like you go through an assembly line, and then you're done." When women spend several hours and several hundred dollars in such a personal venue as a spa, they appreciate a follow-up note offering a future discount, or at least a free product or sample as a thank you.

- *She wants to be treated like a loyal customer, even when she cannot always be one.* "When I got divorced, my ex-husband called my favorite store to stop my charge card, so they called me and said, 'We know you are going through a divorce. You can put it in your name.' They didn't make me explain the whole horrible story."

- *She wants to be accepted at a face value.* "Some of the salespeople think they are better than the shoppers. Or, if you look like you don't have money, or you're not going to buy anything, then why bother with you? I like to shop in my blue jeans. What's with their attitude?"

Lesson 3. Common Sense Should Be the Sixth Sense

The truth about this lesson is that the level of disrespect is so high for so many women that it takes little more than common sense to get a grateful response from them. The littlest things can make a difference. Ask yourself, "Do I treat her with dignity and regard? Do I give her credit for being a smart customer? Am I selling or advertising my product in the place where she is even thinking of me?" For example, do you sell batteries next to where you sell toys? Film near the greeting cards? It is no accident that Wal-Marts have McDonald's inside for harried, hungry moms and kids.

The bookstore Borders used common sense in the way it reconfigured its aisles for children's books. Kids' books are usually placed by chronological reading ages: two and under, two to four, etc. However, so many moms worry that their children are behind their reading ages, and they feel anxious and confused. **Borders reorganized the shelf so that moms can feel good and clear about what to buy, by using their children's own behavior and language to explain: "Read to me," "Read with me," and "Read alone." This is brilliant common sense that respects the way moms think.**

In contrast to these examples, sometimes I am amazed at the blatantly disrespectful things that companies say to the female customers whose money they want. Their behavior is a study in what not to say. Two personal cases in point: I am an enthusiastic spa-aholic. My at-home beauty regimens would pass muster with most advice columns in beauty magazines. So why, when I am lying on the table in a high-end salon, under the bright light and magnifying glass, does the facialist insist on starting the facial not with "Get ready to relax" but with a full-scale investigation? "When was your last facial?" she asks, as if she expects the answer to be "never." Next she starts the sell: "What products are you using now?" Whatever I say, her brusque reply is usually, "That's no good; our products are better for you."

As a final blow, while I am lying under her bright light, feeling really noble about the fact that I am at least trying to improve my skin, she shakes her head and says, "Oh no, you have so much to fix; this will be a lot of work." Her answers make me feel like the salon is a critic, instead of a partner, in beauty.

Here's a training counterpart. I am in good shape, I think, for a woman who has been on the daily work-and-life treadmill at a strong pace. I work out. I don't pig out. And my dancer's bones are still pretty strong. So why, when I showed up at an exercise session at an extremely expensive spa, did the trainer have to say to me, "Do you work out?" Ouch. He could have said, "Tell me about what you do at home," or, "What kind of workout do you usually do?" Would it kill him to think that maybe, though he had yet to whip me into shape, I was trying?

Marketers can learn that the way to a woman's heart and wallet is to trust that she is trying to do the best she can, rather than intimidating her into a sale by adding to her own self-critical list.

How Do You Spell Respect?

L-I-S-T-E-N. In women's eyes, respect starts with listening. Women are always listening, watching for both the nonverbal and the verbal cues that they are important and acknowledged. One woman described the classic jeweler Tiffany this way: "These people take time. They sit down with you, they explain to you about the diamond, where it came from, how big it is, the quality. They stand for quality customer care. It's not the run-of-the-mill, 'Here, I want to sell you this piece so you get out of my face.'"

I remember this woman who spoke about the Tiffany store on New York's Fifth Avenue. Do you know what was interesting about her story? The Tiffany salespeople rarely sit down while they work. Nearly all stand at attention, watching the customers and speaking softly while showing the merchandise. To her, it felt like they were sitting with her alone, carefully taking her by the hand, instead of rushing to the nearest bigger-spending customer. And this tender treatment is not limited to the customers buying diamonds. I have bought low-priced key chains and money clips there and felt like I had made the wisest, most tasteful decision.

Body language and tone of voice are key signals of respect that women can see. A woman sees respect in the way you talk to her, look at her, and take time with her. As one woman said, "I don't want to feel like I have to get what I need really fast because there is a line and the sales clerk doesn't have time to deal with me right now. Make me feel like I'm special."

Paul Higham, former chief marketing officer of Wal-Mart, empathizes with customers this way: "I want to shop in an environment where people are genuinely going to respect me. I don't want to feel like an interruption. Rather, I want to feel as if I am the purpose of their existence."

I learned that lesson early in my career. To earn tuition when I went to college, I worked as a part-time bank teller at Beneficial Savings Bank in Philadelphia for four years. I was taught from day one that although there were teller stools on our side of the window, we had to stand when a customer walked through the revolving door. Even if another teller handled the customer, we were all expected to stand at attention so that we looked eager for people's business. In some of the neighborhoods where I worked, I stood up for people who deposited $5 once a week into a savings account. Stand, smile, look at the passbook, and greet them by name. I guess that is a far cry from tellers today, who often slouch on chairs behind bulletproof windows, and it may be the reason why their electronic surrogates, the more responsive and available

ATMs, have greater appeal. But to me, that training set a standard of the respect I expect. Do you "stand up" for women?

Lesson 4. Respect Her Intelligence; Respect Her Choices

On many levels, today's female consumers are the smartest and most accomplished ever. Fifty-five percent of all BA and MA degrees are awarded to women.[6] More than 60 percent of women work.[7] Sixty-eight percent of women juggle a career and a family.[8] Women own one third of American businesses.[9] Beyond that, women are the beneficiaries of more media, more stimuli, and more access to information than ever before. This is one smart customer—and her life is not easily pegged as a mom or a businesswoman. She lives multiple lives and expects you to respect her in each of her roles. Remembering that can make all the difference.

The travel industry is a place where women's various roles and needs demand respect and seldom get it. Women are extremely exacting and sophisticated travelers, who have historically been overlooked in the largely male business travel segment. Their demands for service link to their demands for respect and validation. Bonnie Reitz of Continental Airlines explained it this way: "When women say they want service, they really want you to recognize that they have chosen to do business with you, and they just want you to acknowledge that and deliver to them what they thought they were purchasing. Women appear to be very methodical in what they choose, and what it is they expect all the way through."

One way that Continental Airlines learns about women's needs is by training their listeners. Bonnie explained, "There is a higher number of women in the entry-level reservations jobs, where women are very comfortable on the phone and tend to be very communicative and sensitive, just by voice, by hearing and understanding. They are more natural as to how they question people, so they give us the information we need to serve them better." Again, it comes back to listening.

Child on Board

An example of role respect in the air is women who travel with children in tow. In one of our discussion groups, a female business traveler admitted, "I know this sounds awful, and I know that they have to go places, but there's nothing worse than traveling near a child." Meanwhile, moms traveling with kids are hypersensitive to the evil eye they get as they work their way down the airplane aisle, carrying a child or two, a car seat, and baggies filled with Cheerios and Game Boys. Has anyone ever asked both groups of female passengers what would work for them? Would some Moms prefer a kids' section so that they can share the stress with other moms? Or would that be the equivalent of a flying crying room? If so, should there be a quiet section for business travelers? The only way to learn how to respect the needs of both groups is to ask.

How about respecting women's need for personal space in the air? Southwest Airlines decided to charge extra for overweight passengers, and the ethics of that are debatable. Having been squished into half of my seat by a neighbor, however, I can see what they were thinking. Do airlines know what really irks many female business travelers? Sprawling seatmates. At the risk of alienating all the polite readers of this book, how many times has the arm rest been hogged by the person next to you? How many times have long legs inched over to your side and suit jackets and newspapers conveniently taken over the precious empty seat between you?

This is the airborne version of the way that many men sit on buses and subways. The airplane seat just costs more and is uncomfortable for a longer trip. American Airlines instituted a new seating configuration that gives coach seats more legroom. How many women would cheer if there were somehow more horizontal room to put an end to cross-country "arm rest-ling"?

As a marketer, think about the self-respect issues of women's roles when you are promoting your product. Moms who fly with children feel unwelcome and labeled as disruptive. Solo female travelers retreat to their rooms rather than endure the cigar smoke and overwhelmingly male lobby bars when they are on the road. Successful marketers need to learn how to regard the different feelings and multiple roles of women and respond to them intelligently.

Care about What She Cares About

If this book had been written five or ten years ago, the idea of cause marketing to build relationships with women would be new. Today, a woman expects that the marketers who earn her dollars will also give some of those dollars to things she cares about. Women will say that given the choice between brand X and brand Y, assuming that the product or service is equal, they will often choose the brand that gives back. The Center for Women's Business Research found that 41 percent of women will switch to brands that are better for the environment, and one in five agree that they choose companies that demonstrate social responsibility.[10] (Incidentally, so many marketers have flocked to breast cancer research that it is difficult for any one brand to own the cause.)

That said, the answer that balances doing the right thing and still getting some credit with women is not necessarily to choose the unheard of, narrow, but interesting cause to differentiate your brand. Women respect companies whose support is consistent, substantial, and ideally interactive with what matters in their lives. Differentiation comes from connecting to causes that are true brand fits and executing events or promotions that are distinctive and reflective of your brand voice.

Lesson 5. Respect What She Cares about in a Way That Also Respects Your Brand Value

Women see right through adopted causes that are really window dressing. When a zillion-dollar company donates half of a percentage of a dollar to a cause, it is disrespectful and can backfire. In addition, be careful that you choose something that makes sense for your brand; otherwise, you may get lost in the cause spotlight shone by bigger players.

One example of cause differentiation by brand is the adoption of breast cancer research by major companies, from Revlon's Fire and Ice Ball to Ford's Race for the Cure to Saks Fifth Avenue's Fashion Targets Breast Cancer, which was reported to raise $9 million in 2002 alone.[11] Avon's Breast Cancer 3-Day Run/Walk, now on its fifth year, has integrated the company's efforts through its global sales force, who have raised $100 million for research through pledges to walkers around the country.[12]

Another cause that gives women appropriate respect is Lifetime's Stop the Violence campaign, which provides awareness for local help centers and domestic abuse hotlines with televised programming and 800 numbers. When Lifetime decided to amp up their efforts in this campaign, Just Ask a Woman conducted research not to ask the obvious question ("Would you feel good if Lifetime led an antiviolence campaign?") but to discover how the brand should talk about it. We interviewed women who were victims of domestic abuse and other sexual crimes to understand the language and images and action that would feel right for them.

Our research groups included victims of violence and women who knew women who had suffered. Sadly, the victims displayed the worst symptoms of the last-in-line mentality that I had ever witnessed. When I asked them to identify which causes were important to them as women, they were at first unwilling even to raise the issue of violence against women. As the session progressed and I gained their trust, I was able to get them to open up about their own experiences. That is how we helped craft legitimate and respectful messages that would include them, not indict them. Getting the message right paid off. Respect women and get respected back.

Another interesting example of finding a brand connection to a cause is 1800Flowers.com's program to fight ovarian cancer. Because the brand is centered on remembering others and creating relationships, the company developed a program for Mother's Day in which women could take their moms to work. For each woman who participated, 1800Flowers.com donated money to the Ovarian Cancer Research Fund. Naturally, the company also sold a particular bouquet during the promotion, which generated additional dollars for the cause. By thinking through unique ways to personalize the cause and make it interactive, 1800Flowers.com demonstrated respect (and not just dollars) for the victims and the victors in the war.

Cracking the Code on Respect

1. *Move her from last in her line to first in yours.* Once you realize how often women are putting everyone else's needs first, look for ways to honor her. Whether it is concierge service or responding quickly to her requests, she will feel the difference.

2. *Interpret respect for your industry, and educate your employees.* The first step to success is to understand what chip may be on her shoulder relative to your category. The next is teaching your relationship staff to anticipate and respond to her needs for respect when she is buying your service.

3. *Common sense should be the sixth sense.* Women are practical beings on whom everyone counts to get things done. When you complicate the buying experience or make simple communications hard, it is particularly annoying to women. She can do it, so why can't you?

4. *Respect her intelligence; respect her choices.* There is no single type of woman. There never was. And thanks to her education and experience, today's female consumer is smarter than ever. Attune yourself and your staff into tailoring products and services to the many lives she juggles.

5. *Respect what she cares about in a way that also respects your brand value.* Cause marketing is now a price of entry in marketing with women. Differentiating your programs, creating interactivity, and getting real-world participation for women is key. Be sure that the program is something only your brand can do.

When women feel they are respected by your brand, they can choose you comfortably and stay with you. As I said in Chapter 2, simplifying her busy life is one of the best brand benefits you can give her. That brings her a little closer to her personal goal—some time for herself. The desire to seek comfort and restore peace of mind and a sense of home is very powerful for women.

This book began with women's quest for time. The next chapter reveals how women seek serenity through the pleasure of being with friends and family, as well as the ultimate gift: time alone. How can you, as a marketer, tap into this urge to nest and rest without invading her personal space? The next chapter tells the story.

CHAPTER
8

Craving
Comfort

Sometimes I just wish someone would take care of me.

In addition to my career as a marketer, I speak to women around the country about achieving balance in their day-to-day lives. So many women are looking for a way out or up or away from the pressures and stresses they sometimes put on themselves. I always share with them the story of my *Mirror Test*.

The Mirror Test was a technique I invented to sort out my priorities when I headed the N. W. Ayer & Partners advertising agency. At the end of the day, I would literally or figuratively look in the mirror and ask myself three questions to judge my performance on what I thought were the most important issues of my job. Did I do the right things for the people in the agency? Did I do the right thing for our clients? Did I do my best for the advertising work itself? If I could answer "yes" to all three, I gave myself permission to get a good night's sleep, which rarely came anyway because of the long and often-stressful days.

It was not until I took a break from the roller-coaster pace of that role that I learned that I had forgotten a key question for the mirror: "Did I do the right thing for Mary Lou today?" When I tell that story to audiences, I see relief and hope in women's eyes. While women gladly devote time to their families and their jobs, that self-imposed last-in-line position can wear them out. It is a kind of plague for overachievers. Nonetheless, they are also incredibly resilient. With a little inspiration from an article or a speech, and perhaps from you as a marketer, they can begin to deal with their resistance to rest and start to create oases of comfort in their lives.

In the last chapter I discussed how women put themselves last in line. This chapter turns the tables on that notion. Women, who are self-reliant and proud of their ability to handle everything, are also learning to know when to fold 'em. They are discovering that they cannot depend on anyone else to give them a break, so they have taken on their own comfort and restoration as an underground crusade.

Marketers in the comfort industries, such as furnishings, decor, soft goods, and do-it-yourself wares, as well as entertainment, spa, food, and leisure travel, will find lessons for capitalizing on this truth. I believe that every business has something to learn from the power of what comfort means to women. Just as stress is a negative filter for the way women view your product or service, *comfort craving* is a positive force that can influence what you sell and how you treat her. This chapter provides advice for capturing the comforts and security of home—through messages, environment, and experience—without rubbing in the traditional domestic life she has moved beyond.

From the growth of book clubs to the transformation of neighborhood beauty parlors into day spas, from massages going mass to aromatherapy in dishwashing liquid, the rush is on to relax.

 As a marketer, is women's search for personal restoration and care something that your brand can or should tap into? Is there a way that your product or service can serve

up a little comfort as a benefit? Do you understand where a woman draws the line between restorative nurturing and new-age hooey? This chapter lets you in on her secret craving and shows you the right way to satisfy her hunger. The lessons start with the home itself, its meanings and relevance for women, and then expand to women's indulgence in treats and their retreat to spas, and finally unearth women's often unspoken desire—solitary confinement, namely, some time to themselves.

There's No Place Like Home

A wonderful ad for Citibank in New York City was posted to the side of a building I pass every day on my way home. The ad said, "There's a reason most people don't have a picture of their office at home. Live richly."

This theme particularly resonated with me, as it would with many busy women. In 1998 I became a kind of poster child for the overly agenda-filled working woman who decided to fold 'em. As I mentioned earlier, I had been CEO of a large ad agency for five years and had been working hard for 23 years straight. That year, I just needed a break. I decided to take an unprecedented five weeks off that I called a Walkabout—really a totally work-free vacation to reevaluate my priorities. Mostly, I stayed home and enjoyed my New York neighborhood for the first time. I kept a daily journal and wrote about the experience, and I began to speak to women's groups around the country about the value of self-assessment and taking a break. I often told of the elation I felt on the first morning I was able to wake up and drink a cup of coffee while sitting in the sunshine in my own living room, instead of rushing to work. That ordinary moment was a blinding glimpse of the obvious need to balance the excitement of a career with the peace of home.

Women I have interviewed quickly differentiate between a house and a home. A house is a temporary living space, a place in which to fall asleep and put your things. Home is the name a woman gives to the place she loves most—not because it is grand or lasting but because it is hers. As a woman said to me, "A house is just a building. Your home is you." I know that my home is me.

Our House Is a Very, Very, Very Fine House

I spend my weekdays living in an apartment in New York City's East Village. It looks homey, but it is undoubtedly a city dwelling. On the weekends, my husband Joe, my dog Danny, and I escape to a small farmhouse in Bucks County, Pennsylvania. Since Joe and I both come from Pennsylvania, there is a going-home feeling, even to the roads that lead to it. This little house is purposely decorated in the simplest, most calming colors and style. This feeling comes from the sensual texture of the house, the smell of flowers and old wood, the sun coming through the kitchen, the crickets at night, and even the old furniture and retro touches that shield this house from the twenty-first century and make it mine. I dream of the comfort of that house. I live for it. And that weekend peace of mind has made it possible for me to stay in love with New York City for 25 years.

Women's descriptions of their homes range from humorous to touching, and they are always a glimpse into everyday life. As one woman said, "My home is like a day care center. It's where the kids hang out. We play hard there, and we entertain a lot of the time. My husband constantly reminds me that it's a gift that kids want to hang around with us, but sometimes I wish the gifts weren't here so often."

For women who have happy home lives, through family or friendships, home is a safe place where they can let go and be themselves. One woman described it this way: "A home is somewhere you can go to be protected, kind of a retreat." It is interesting to contrast the chaos of modern lives and the challenge of creating a retreat, but for many women home is as much an emotional concept as it is a residence. Stressed women crave the comfort of home.

Just Ask Donata Maggipinto, Culinary and Entertaining Director of Williams-Sonoma . . .

Donata Maggipinto wears many hats. She is not only the culinary and entertaining director of Williams-Sonoma but also the author of books such as Real-Life Entertaining *and a frequent guest on cooking and entertaining topics on the* Today Show. *Donata shared with me her philosophy of home life: "I always laugh about the idea of 'cocooning' as a trend. I don't think that it is a trend because women have always enjoyed spending time in their homes. We can go out and try to be superwomen, hold these jobs and volunteer, and be really busy, but I think at the core—and this is such a wonderful, almost sacred thing— women are nesters. We are caretakers. We like to take care of our families and our homes. In a post 9/11 time of world trauma, everybody went home and stayed home. I know that one of the reasons that our sales at Williams-Sonoma are so positive is because people are spending more time at home, cooking at home, where they feel safe and secure." If, as a marketer, you are envisioning soft-focused pictures of families gathered around the hearth enjoying peace and quiet, think again.*

Lesson 1. Define Comfort the Way She Does—Personally and Creatively

Try to avoid the overused scenes of women sitting cross-legged in yoga repose. Women sense comfort in the nuances of a quiet moment, even in the middle of a crazy day. It is more important that you link your product or service to the real benefits of comfort: peace of mind, easy enjoyment, and simplicity of access and use.

More Real Life than Real Perfect

First of all, most women are proud to describe their homes as comfortable rather then beautiful, such as, "Friends will tell me they feel comfortable in my home. They know they can come in and curl up on the sofa and kick off their shoes." Another woman described her furniture as "if it's not stained, it's not used.'" A recent print campaign for a flooring company takes advantage of this messy comfort by showing a beautiful floor covered with spilled milk and a sprawling dog. It still looks beautiful, but it feels comfortable, as well.

In the decorating arena, I have heard women describe extremes of behavior. One woman told me her house is a "never-ending story." She said that she constantly experiments with new painting techniques, from sponge to faux Roman ruins, so that every room is completely different. Another women bragged about changing her color scheme every season. One told me that she actually decorated a Christmas tree in every room, even the bathrooms. What was important to nearly all the women I interviewed on this topic was that their homes were personal expressions of their creativity and reflections of the state of their own life needs.

Women I have spoken with contrast their homes with the homes they grew up in, such as this woman's memory: "My home is truly a home. It's well lived in. Unlike my mom, I have no rooms that I use as a showpiece. Every room is one you can relax and be comfortable in." Another explained, "My mother is very traditional. I grew up in a house with big claw and ball feet antiques. Nothing could ever be left out. Shoes had to go in the closet, or she had a conniption. I can't live with that kind of control." Most women have abandoned standards of perfection and replaced them with a more casual approach to cooking, entertaining, and decorating.

I can remember the house where I grew up in Philadelphia as easy living versus elegant. I had friends who had living rooms filled with fancy white French provincial furniture covered in plastic slipcovers and plastic runners that protected the carpet from little feet. I remember thinking that their Moms were too fussy for my taste and that somehow our simpler row house was the easier way to grow up. During my childhood there were few home-baked cookies, crafts lessons, and dinner parties because my mom worked. That may not seem strange, but it was the 1960s, and those touches were a bigger deal then. But my mom was happy, and that was good enough for my dad, my brother Jack, and me.

While an ideal homemaker of the past might have been expected to be equally adept at cooking, cleaning, decorating, and entertaining, the women I have interviewed on the subject pick and choose what they are best at.

Marketers in the home categories should recognize that women blend creativity with practicality and that a perfectly decorated bedroom may be in the same home as a kitchen with nothing but take-out food inside. And that's OK with them. Women just cannot be separated into two camps of home fanaticism and home ambivalence. There are too many shades of gray in between.

Donata Maggipinto believes that the best a marketer in the home-related categories can do is to help relieve lingering perfectionist traps that some women feel: "Perfection is something that brings two certainties for women: frustration and exhaustion." In the advice she gives to her readers, she says, "You can't be perfect. Life isn't perfect and that's the beauty of it. Accept that your home is a little bit messy. It's okay as long as you're happy with it. Live your life the way it matters to you."

Ages and Stages

Different groups of women at different stages of life adapt home to their current needs. Moms with kids tell me that they are used to the never-ending stream of neighborhood kids, backyard barbeques, and potluck dinners. Newly divorced women described martini parties and Friday night margaritas and Mexican food take-out. Women who are alone again (after the kids leave or after a divorce or the death of a spouse) are a huge target for home decor and entertaining products because many can at last reset the table to their own liking.

Some women in their 40s and 50s experience an emotional release when the kids are grown and out of the house, especially after so many years of cooking and keeping a home for others. One woman who was still waiting for her freedom said, "They come in one door and out the other. My youngest is still home. I'll be 60 in February and have yet to experience empty-nest syndrome. I guess when they put me in a nursing home, I'll finally know what it's like." Another woman credited her newfound solitude to the joy of doing things for herself: "I've just decided in my golden years to treat myself really nice. I keep my table set, and whatever the meal is, whether it's peanut butter and jelly, I want it laid out special, just for me."

The marketing value of this segment comes from the combination of their increased wealth and their desire to spend on themselves. Their willingness to experiment and express their own personalities after so many years of conforming to the otherness of what is best for the family makes them a fantastic target for marketers. You might recall the humorous commercial from a home improvement center that began with the middle-aged couple waving goodbye to their college-bound son, only to whiz up to his bedroom to start measuring for the new Jacuzzi they plan to install. That euphoria is an entirely new opportunity for smart marketers, and it could apply as easily to the young woman with her first apartment and the recent divorcee who is ready to toss the Barcalounger.

Lesson 2. Utilize Life-Stage Segmentation, but Link It Uniquely to Comfort Benefits

After listening to women break every preconception, with their pick-and-choose approach to the home arts, I recommend that marketers consider segmenting messages by comfort benefits such as reward, self-expression, and community to attract and connect with various groups of women, instead of limiting themselves to age or lifestyle targeting. This provides a way to bridge the real reasons why women buy and do things for their homes, as well as to avoid the stereotypes of the on-the-go careerist versus the nurturing, homebound mom.

The major home improvement chains, such as Home Depot and Lowe's Home Improvement Warehouse, have recognized the economic power of women in their categories and the retail barriers to buying their products. In a national survey of female homeowners commissioned by Lowe's, 94 percent of all female homeowners claimed to be do-it-yourselfers, completing a home improvement project themselves in the last five years. Additionally, 57 percent of single female house owners classified themselves as intermediate or better in their skills. Of most interest to marketers in this segment, 80 percent of home improvement projects were initiated by women.[1]

Male readers might smile at this thought if they have ever heard their female partner muse about how nice it would be if X were fixed or Y were improved. Female readers probably visualize the next "to do" on your own improvement lists. My colleague Tracy Brogan tells the story of her engaged girlfriend who declared her first married to-dos: "Our first project will be to resand the kitchen floor. Our first purchase will be the Jacuzzi for the deck."

Today, most women are not waiting for the men in their lives to pick up the hammer and the paintbrush. They are buying the power drills, the lumber, the tile, and the hardware to get it done for their own pleasure and, on some level, their own empowerment and satisfaction.

Women in the survey also indicated how much they would like home improvement tools and items as gifts, how they wish that tools were more ergonomically designed for their use, and how much they want to learn how-to techniques and decorating ideas from an authoritative source. This is a far cry from the warehouses of pick-and-go, no-questions-asked building supply centers of the past. Did Home Depot and Lowe's ever know they would be in the business of helping women build comfort in their homes? Both chains have been offering classes in everything from installing toilets to tile, and the results have fueled tremendous sales growth.

It's not just about building things to enhance a home's comfort; it's also about buying them. Recognizing women's growing appreciation for design and quality at every price level, stores like Target have been able to introduce the Michael Graves and Phillipe Starck lines of home wares to great success. Pottery Barn and Crate and Barrel have created full-room inspiration by selling everything from custom upholstery to matching picture frames.

The Big Picture

In the past couple of years, a brand new concept—the superstores of home design and improvement, namely, Home Depot's EXPO and The Great Indoors—has capitalized on an important insight that traditional home improvement stores have missed.

The layout of the typical home store, whether Wal-Mart or Home Depot, separates the big items (like beds or bathtubs) from the accessories like towels or sheets. Shower curtains and window treatments are placed far away from the essential details like the custom drawer knobs or bedside tables. Stores compartmentalize, which is closer to the male decision-making pattern of eliminating options to decide. As described earlier, anthropological theories indicate that women integrate all the pieces, and that their ability to see in full color and detail calls for a different kind of floor layout and merchandising to sell full-room renovation. If a woman has to pick up the towel, carry it to the bathtub section, and then match it to a piece of wallpaper on the other side of the floor, she is doing all the work herself. The Great Indoors displays everything in one space, the way she thinks. Products are arranged by entire room sets, with all the appliances, fabrics, and soft goods put together in context. That kind of marketing understands how women decide.

Lesson 3. Reposition Your Business from Selling Renovation to Designing Comfort

When women are turning their energy to their homes, the buying and usage experience should be as comfortable as the end result. The point is not to make the tools pink or add lounge areas to the lumberyard but to organize and label the merchandise so that it follows a woman's logic and is thus easy to buy. It's about how the salespeople share their knowledge and advice in store and in seminars. Also important is your continued relationship building, through the access and information that she can consult afterward, whether printed, online, or through other demonstration-inspiration media such as magazines and sponsored do-it-yourself shows on TV.

That TV shows such as *Trading Spaces*, *Christopher Lowell*, and *Painted House* are runaway hits tells you that women love the vicarious "What I would do?" angle of decorating as much as the how-to story. Women are inspired as much by the transformation as by the linear step-by-step. Think beauty makeover in brick and fabric, and you get the picture.

The most popular makeover candidate for comfort is the bathroom. Bathrooms have surpassed kitchens as the most frequently remodeled home in the house. Understanding the way women experience the bath adds up to a huge marketing opportunity and is the difference between being in the renovation business and the comfort design business. Women are not just seeking new Formica countertops. They are designing home spas and roomy shower and steam rooms and enlarging the space to accommodate working out and relaxing, instead of just washing up. And what is a bathroom without the requisite piles of towels, rows of aromatherapy candles, and even his and her terry robes to make the spa feeling complete?

Renovation is also a category where women look to other women (their boards of directors) for advice. The Lowe's survey indicated that 75 percent of women turn to friends for advice on where to go and what to buy. The way you treat each woman in this category kick starts your own positive or negative buzz marketing campaign. Think of each woman in your showroom as representing a dozen others, and you are in business.

A product idea to attract women that is much simpler than creating a whole new store concept is to use new packaging, like that from Dutch Boy paint. With women doing home improvement work, and particularly regarding their role in choosing the colors of the room, you would think that a paint company would have invented a way to make painting more female-friendly. Dutch Boy introduced a new paint can that has three advantages. First, it is lighter because it is plastic. Second, it has a twist-off top, so it is easier to open. Third, it has a spout for easy pouring. The commercial features three fashionable women twisting and pouring, and although the copy never says that it is for women, it is pretty obvious. The truth of this product improvement is that by listening to women, the company made a better product for men as well. Whoever said that men preferred heavy, dripping, metal cans that are hard to open, anyway?

Turning Ritual to Revenue

Another area of creating comfort that also creates new marketing opportunities is women's interest in perpetuating family rituals and traditions. For some women, holidays are a chance to replicate their childhood memories for their own children. Again, Donata Maggipinto weighs in: "Holiday traditions are really significant.

Rituals are reenacted every year; cookies are baked; the same or-naments are unwrapped; and the same guests are sitting around the table. The rituals around the holidays are fun, but they are also important."

Women derive comfort from these rituals, and the home en-tertaining industries have capitalized on them. As a marketer, however, there is a deeper learning to be found from the concept of a ritual that stretches beyond the periodic holidays. The repet-itive nature of rituals can enhance everyday living and restoration for women. For instance, yoga and massage practices are inher-ently peaceful because of a series of repeated and perfected steps, poses, and moves. Many women find solace in the ritual of laying out the yoga mat, lighting the candle, playing relaxing music, and perfecting the moves. How could the sensual quality of these ritu-als be transformed into new product ideas for the home?

One category that has benefited from this home ritual is dec-orative pillows. How many beds—especially in the woman's bedroom—have you seen stacked with small, decorative pillows? What are all those pillow for? If your house has them, you know that every night, all those pillows are put away, only to be restaged on the remade bed in the morning. What is that all about? There is a ritual about creating a beautiful bed, even if it is inconvenient for day-to-day living. It may not be true in every room in the house, but the piling up of fluffy or pretty pillows on beds is a sym-bol of a haven, not just a sleeping place. I wonder if it hearkens back to childhood beds piled with teddy bears and dolls, which made the bed a nighttime home? (Just a little self-therapy from this admitted pillow stacker.)

Put a Little Zen in the Wash

Just how far can a marketer take this interest in the rituals of com-fort? An unlikely candidate for romancing a ritual might seem to be dishwashing liquid. Most women converted long ago to electric dishwashers to get that chore off their list. But there are always the random dishes, glasses, pots, and pans that call for washing by hand. Williams-Sonoma understood that the chore of dishwashing could be looked at as a positive ritual if the products brought some sensual joy to the user. Enter the Essential Oils collection, with aromatherapy fragrances like Meyer Lemon and Rosemary Basil. As Donata Maggipinto describes it, "You can take a ritual like washing dishes, and make it into time that is personally satisfying to you, so that you will derive more pleasure from it. I'm doing the dishes, and I'm engaging all my senses, smelling the wonderful aroma of basil; the essential oil in the liquid is kinder to my hands, and all of a sudden a chore becomes kind of what I call 'meditative moments.'" These meditative moments can also come from the company's window wash, countertop wash, and floor cleaner. It may sound bizarre, but I bought the dishwashing liquid and displayed it next to the sink on a little silver tray usually reserved for table wine because its simple package is so well designed. It even converts me, a dishwashing-machine brat, into a hand washer.

A Dose of Comfort Every Day

Comfort comes in the little things. Home catalogs from Domestications, the Company Store, Garnet Hill, and Cuddledown soften the edges of modern living. The last couple of years have favored coverlets to toss casually over chairs, throw rugs to warm up floors, and enough bath oils, soaps, candles, and automated, water-dripping fountains to create a sanctuary in a townhouse. You can find small stones for the garden with "peace" and "contentment" carved into their surfaces, wind chimes that bring native Indian or Asian harmony to the porch, and feng shui kits for instant karma. Mail-order peace of mind is yours for the asking.

Players in the home furnishings and appliances industry have found ways to place their products within the emotional security context that women see them. For example, an ad for Bernhardt sofas takes the shape of a sofa and fills it with handwriting that promises, "This is not just my sofa. It is a way of telling you who I am. It says I like nice things, not fussy things. It says I am comfortable with who I am. It says I want you to be comfortable, too." Clearly, Bernhardt recognizes the psychology of the couch purchase in a big way, although I'm not sure I'm ready for a sofa with an identity crisis.

Even a chilly modern steel refrigerator can join the comfort brigade. An ad for Amana shows a casually dressed, happy woman carrying ice cream out of the kitchen. The headline says, "5 girlfriends. *Sleepless in Seattle* on DVD. This is no time to lose the ice cream in the back of the freezer." The body copy explains the Easy Reach feature that organizes the refrigerator, although the photo of the product is secondary to the focus on the happy girlfriend. It's about easy time together, not about counting the freezer drawers.

Nothin' Says Lovin' Like . . .

In the spirit of acknowledging that women cherry-pick their preferred bit of home keeping, I want to admit that I am no cook. Thankfully, I am married to Joe, who is a talented one, or we would starve.

Some women have segmented their love-hate for cooking based on whether it is a necessity or a pleasure. A woman in one of my sessions said, "I would say that cooking wasn't in my contract when I got married. I don't want someone to tell me you need to cook. I enjoy cooking when I want to cook."

Other women boast of just how little skill they can get away with, such as, "I've learned that pretty much everything on earth can be put on the Foreman Grill." Another confessed, "I'm not really Betty Crocker. I'm more like Elly May Clampett" (the naive country daughter from the *Beverly Hillbillies*). Another woman described her favorite meal as a New Year's fondue: "It eliminates me from being in the kitchen all day, and if you don't like the way the meat's done, it's your fault because you cooked it."

Other women do find joy in it, perhaps as a release from office life or as an expression of love and creativity. As one woman told me, "I have a friend who teases me, 'Miss Martha Stewart, what are you preparing for your family today?'" Another agreed, "I go to bed cooking, and I wake up cooking. When I'm at work, I'll go through the websites to look for the recipe of the day so I have some clue of what to cook for dinner that night."

Referring back to the decision resources I described in Chapter 3, the avid cook's board of directors includes celebrity chefs on the ever-expanding food channel to websites and magazines to her friends and relatives. Emeril Lagasse and Sara Moulton have become household names, and the Food Network has made gourmet cooking accessible.

Tomato Soup and Grilled Cheese

Comfort food is one of the earlier labels that connected retro foods like meatloaf and macaroni and cheese to the emotional level of home and Mom, but the fever to jump on the comfort bandwagon has only increased after the events of September 11, 2001. Despite reports of the growing girth of Americans, food marketers recognize the potent role that food has in restoring emotional comfort. At the mass level, unlike the Creamette noodles and Velveeta that my Mom mixed to make the dish, today Lipton translates the concept to premade cheese-and-noodle dishes for grownups. Outside the home, the comfort food trend continues with the new Ian Schrager property, the redesigned Hudson Hotel in New York City, which features different varieties of mac and cheese as the cornerstone of its menu. The trend to comfort extends to the revival of diner food across the country. Even party caterers are serving up miniburgers, baby BLTs, and cocktail franks for a feel-good atmosphere. The emotional value of food should not be underestimated, especially for busy, stressed women.

When you think of coffee, you might think of a shot of caffeine from the local Starbucks. But coffee has been expanding from its wake-up energizer role to a lineup of calming, creamy coffee drinks that have become addictive afternoon respites from the office, such as their Frappucino and Caramel Macchiato. The Frappucino business alone accounts for $1 billion worth of sales from a portfolio of products, including the served beverage, bottled versions, and ice cream bars sold in grocery stores. The sweetness and the momentary escape from the desk add up to workday comfort for many busy women in a somewhat healthier version of a cigarette break.

Co-opting comfort can get dicey for marketers. It's a no-brainer when a product like Cascadian Farms' organic macaroni and cheese runs an ad with the headline "Pure Comfort," but how about when Hormel Sausages bills its wieners as "nirvana"? In a 2002 print ad, a beautifully fit woman bends in a yoga position under the headline "Stress-free day" followed by the copy, "It's a day to clear your mind. A day to free your soul. And a day for Hormel Always Tender honey mustard pork loin filet." This pork promise might challenge nutritional logic, but Hormel took the proposition a step further with a second ad that connects the benefit of "no worry" to selling bacon.

Women have a complex relationship with food. It is solace for stress. It is guilt-ridden for those counting calories. And it is tied back to that internal tug-of-war that she has with the mirror: to indulge or not? To be thin or happy?

Just Ask Betta Gallego, Vice President of Marketing, Dole Packaged Foods . . .

Someone who understands women's relationship with food is Betta Gallego, Vice President of Marketing for the Dole Packaged Foods Division, responsible for all canned fruits and juices as well as snacks and a product called Fruit Bowls®. Betta explained how she feels women view food: "It fulfills at least two different needs. It's the fuel to do what they want to do in their lives and it's the way they escape and find comfort. Women look at their food as a series of trade offs. She has a number of calories she can't exceed, so she wants to maximize the satisfaction. To learn what that satisfaction means to her, it's important to probe deeply to understand the psyche of women. For instance, we tested a concept board that showed women trading off between a donut and a carrot. It's not realistic for women. They said, that if a woman wanted a donut, there was no way she's was going to eat a carrot at that very moment. Marketers need to understand the nuances for them to connect."

Ahhhh Spas

Before I share women's desire for spa and well-being experiences, I want to admit my own fixations in this area. I have indulged in massages around the world from hot-stone therapy to Irish thallasotherapy to underwater Japanese watsu. I have had facials made of pulverized nightingale droppings (not kidding) and had my feet pedicured with rose petals. At the Miraval Spa outside Tucson, I went through the "equine experience"—a horse-whisperer kind of session where under the guise of getting in touch with your feelings, you clean a horse's hooves. (It works.) I have drawers full of candles and crystals and aromatherapy products from friends. My Tarot cards have been read, and my cranium has been rubbed. So, I have a grip on—or at least an addiction to—what is happening in this category.

That is why I am not surprised when I ask women what they

would most like as a reward for their business; often, a day at a spa comes up spontaneously. Once the privilege of the well-heeled consumer, the broadening array of spa services, especially massage, has increased the exposure and interest in the category. Spa comfort is the ultimate luxury; as one woman described it, "Luxury for me is doing things for myself that I didn't do in the past, because I can now. I go to the spa regularly for massages, facials, things that I really enjoy."

Consumers spend between $4 and $6 billion annually on visits to massage therapists,[2] and the number of massages is growing. According to the American Massage Therapy Association, 17 percent of American adults had a massage in 2001—twice the level of 1997.[3] Maybe the increasing stress in women's lives is the reason; maybe it is that you can get a massage anywhere from a spa to a booth at the mall. I think it is something more fundamental: We need to be touched and comforted.

Just ask Bob Goehrke, Vice President of Bath and Body Works . . .

Bob Goehrke is a marketing vice president of The Limited's Bath and Body Works. He believes that excellence in this category starts with great products but requires a great retail experience as well: "When a customer walks through the mall, she's pushing a stroller, everything's blaring at her. She's searching for a shopping oasis. We have a high level of trust and loyalty with our customers, and they come in often. When she steps into our store, it's not unusual that someone knows her by name, and says, 'How about if I give you a two-minute hand massage?' It may be the first time she was touched all day by a human being. There's that whole sense of discovery. She can look at all the products, enjoy the aromatherapy. There's always something new. There's no pressure to buy. The average time women stay in our stores is almost 45 minutes, which is a long time for our business."

It is interesting that Bath and Body Works is rolling out an expansion of a concept store now operating in their home base of Columbus, Ohio. This 8,000-square-feet store not only sells products but also offers spa services such as massages, pedicures, and fragrance and aromatherapy rooms so that customers can experience the products on site. Bob said that its convenience and attitude reflect the brand's accessible personality: "You can come into a Bath and Body Works and be pampered. No tipping. No waiting in long lines."

TLC and Me

When women go to a spa for a treatment or a day of beauty, they turn over their egos as well as their bodies for a little loving care. My experience has taught me, however, that the spa services business, while regulated for health and cleanliness practices, could use a little training in the area of customer comfort. It is funny that when you get a massage or facial, sometimes there is a little sign with "spa etiquette" that lists your obligations as a customer, such as taking a shower beforehand and suggested tipping. How about an etiquette policy that works in reverse? Remember that story I told in Chapter 7 about being asked when I had had my last facial and then having all those products thrust at me?

Again, a spa is not just about the treatments. It is about the environment, the personal attention, the unrushed time, and the focus on her and only her. Other industries have enhanced their real estate to capture the pampering that women crave.

Lesson 4. Comfort Is Not a List of Rational Benefits; It Is a Touch, a Validation, and a Shared Respect

The spa and beauty industries have developed every kind of innovative treatment, product, experience, and escape. The wellness segment continually reaches out to new therapies for mind and body. But how much care has been put into employee training to ensure that women's unspoken needs for validation are delivered? A friend describes going for a pedicure this way: "I need to be touched." That is more important than the newest alpha-hydroxy skin emollient.

The cosmetics industry is rife with entire brands dedicated to comfort and calmness. Origins' skin and body products like Peace of Mind, Philosophy's hair conditioner Sheer Contentment, and the entire Aveda line and Bath and Body Works Well-Being Solutions Center are comfort personified. One of the biggest recent fragrance introductions in years was Clinique's Happy. Estee Lauder president Dan Brestle summed up its conception this way: "It was launched in 1997, when people started to feel good about themselves again. All the popular brands then had a dark side to them, a kind of heroin chic. The market was starting to take off, and there was a lot of optimism: Let the good times roll. And Happy was the right thing for the Clinique brand." That eau de optimism is still holding strong: Happy is ranked a number-one fragrance, particularly among young women.

Comfort to Go

Another industry that has learned firsthand the escalating importance of providing comfort is the airline industry. Bonnie Reitz, senior vice president for sales and marketing at Continental Airlines, hailed the company's President's Club as particularly valued by women: "All customers like our President's Club. It's the safe, quiet haven away from all the chaos and rushing around. Women really appreciate it because it gives them a little bit of privacy, a feeling that they are being recognized as the important travelers they are. They seem to be more appreciative of the detailing in the clubs. They notice that that we have created the bar area with panel dividers to keep the noise level down. We have nice group seating so people can have an intimate conversation. Family rooms so that families can get together. Women lock on that we are trying to make the travel experience much better."

Another place that women find refuge is in their cars. They can be a source of comfort and escape and the ultimate luxury: time alone. While women typically talk first about the importance of physical safety in automotive vehicles, they quickly gravitate to features that provide "car-cooning." I have heard women go on and on about seat warmers, leather upholstery, stereo sound systems, buttons that automatically align the seats and mirrors to their specs, and the in-car peacekeeper, separate climate controls. Their cars are often the one place they can escape, since as one woman said, "Reality is there again once you pull into your driveway." A young mom explained, "Being in my car is the only time I really have to be by myself, between work and kids. I can do what I want; I can have the stereo playing; it's my time for myself." An older woman rejoiced, "It's just me on one seat and my purse on the other."

All by Myself

Although many women can find comfort with others, I often hear about the ultimate source of comfort, which is delicious time alone.

One of the most absolute proclamations I heard on this came from a woman who described it this way: "I feel my emotionally healthiest right now. The kids are gone, the husband is gone, the dog, the cat, the bird, and I'm alone and loving life." The other women in the group session almost stood to applaud.

She was not the only one who wanted some time alone. Sometimes women say they have to be sick just to get it. A woman shared this story: "There was the time that I got strep throat. I felt awful, and there was nothing to do but go to bed for two days. I got a couple of books I hadn't read, and I have to say, they were the best two days I could remember." Another woman looked to her retirement as a time when she could finally get some solitary time: "The only time I'm going to feel good is when I am 67 and I stop working. I can just do whatever I want, like paint and swim in my pool and just not care about anyone else."

As one woman said when I asked her what she deserved, "I deserve a week by myself in my own house." Relating back to the concept of otherness from Chapter 7, women have little time for themselves after they have given it all away to everyone else.

Seeking Solitary Confinement

The media has seen tremendous revenue from recent launches in comfort-directed content and programming. Oprah Winfrey's O magazine, which is an astounding success, helps women deal with issues like developing spirituality, finding time for themselves, and resolving conflicts. Each issue includes a photo of a remote, natural setting for women to imagine the peace of being there, away from daily life.

Cathie Black, president of Hearst Magazines, describes Oprah's success this way: "People have always admired Oprah Winfrey. We were able to take that energy and inspiration and translate that into the pages of a magazine. The quality of the magazine, the pages, the photographs—it is almost like a gift to women to say, 'We respect you; we admire you.' Women learn from it. If they want a better life, they learn how to start. And even if they don't, it values what they do."

Cathie sees magazines giving women back the comfort and restoration they seek: "By the time a woman is finally relaxing at the end of an evening, sitting in bed, just a chance to spend 25 minutes with a magazine, it's like taking a big breath of fresh air, almost as if with a friend. And in the world that we live in today, that magazine better be very carefully edited, because that woman is parceling out those extra minutes she has in that day. You'd better appeal to her; she has lots of other places she can spend that time."

Real Simple magazine, launched by Time Inc. in 2000 and sold under a theme developed by Just Ask a Woman ("Do Less. Have More.") has included dozens of articles on how to find quiet time, organize for serenity, and escape to new lifestyles. The concept clicked, and *Real Simple* was named best magazine of the year by Advertising Age.

Lesson 5. Leave Her Alone

Women love spending time with family and friends, but they also need to be in their own space to regroup from their busy lives and to be released from the demands of others. Think of that the next time you create a sweepstakes for busy moms, with the reward of a week in Disney World with the family. Otherness may motivate her to enter, but if she wins, she might prefer to disappear to a desert spa instead.

Whether it is spending time with family or friends, improving the comfort of their nests, or seeking relief outside the home in spas or retreats, women still need some self-elected solitary confinement. As marketers, it is important to remember this unspoken wish for privacy and quiet time.

Many marketers are taking the easy route of borrowing images of serenity, such as pictures of women doing yoga to personify their product, the language of Zen, or the music of Enya pulsing through their sales pitches. The important thing is to deliver it.

An ad for Tylenol PM showed a woman in an arched yoga position, with the headline, "This morning was brought to you by a good night's sleep," followed by the brand's tagline, "For great mornings, take comfort in our strength." The promise and the visual are believable together. A print ad for the Balance Collection by Marika takes a manifesto approach to the company's relaxed workout apparel. The copy reads, "The challenge for today's modern women is to find a Balance between the demands of motherhood, job, household, society, and her own personal being. What she wears goes a long way to help free her of the tension and stress that come with life's responsibilities." The words are a little lofty for a T-shirt, but the empathy for comfort clothes for her pursuit of balance is right on.

Does your product or service really help her find comfort in her home, her relationships, and her mind? Is it relaxing to buy you, to interact with you online or on the phone? Do you give her a feeling of security and safety when she experiences you?

Cracking the Code on Comfort

1. *Define comfort the way she does—personally and creatively.* Do not jump on the clichés. Look for how women can find comfort in the realistic small ways that you can deliver—a calm environment, an unhurried pace, and gracious service.

2. *Utilize life-stage segmentation, but link it uniquely to comfort benefits.* Remember that there are take-out moms and cooking singles. Look for what they share in common—a need for reward and some time with their feet up, surrounded by pals.

3. *Reposition your business from selling renovation to designing comfort.* Even the hardest-core do-it-yourselfers are doing it for a reason. They are trying to create environments they love. Build that promise into your tool kits.

4. *Comfort is not a list of rational benefits; it is a touch, a validation, and a shared respect.* The temptation might be to jump on com-

fort as a buzzword or a trend, but the point is not to borrow the language of wellness and serenity. You must deliver real benefits and services that actually bring some comfort into her life.

5. *Leave her alone*. Women are the first ones to fill their days with other people's needs. Look for ways you can help her clear out time for herself. You can build spaces for privacy into your store, products that are single-serve treats for her, and apparel that is a pleasure for her to wear on her own time.

Women are triumphant, powerful, other-focused beings. They can handle a tremendous amount of stress, especially when it is necessary to safeguard their families and friends. As a marketer, can you find a way to alleviate that stress, to put her first, to ease her decision making and shopping and her connections off- and online—and can you do it with respect? If you can, you will be the marketer who wins the hearts of women and truly cracks the code of success.

These past seven chapters have deciphered the code on key issues and behaviors of today's female consumers. The challenge for you as a marketer is to link these truths to your own company and culture. The next chapter sums up a series of action steps, lessons learned, and the best recommendations from other marketing executives and women themselves for cracking the code of what women want.

CHAPTER 9

A Listening
Action Plan
for Marketers

Now what?

Now that you have listened to the key issues on women's minds, you may be looking for some very specific ideas on how to make listening to women part of your everyday marketing life.

This chapter sums up several major areas where you can make an immediate difference but also captures mid- and longer-term ways to begin marketing with women. In addition, true to the form of the Just Ask a Woman interviews, I invited female consumers to weigh in with some final words of wisdom.

Fast-Track Your Listening Skills Development

In the first chapter you tested your female IQ with a checkup of often-heard statements about marketing to women. Now it is time to rethink the kind of processes you can put in place to improve your checkup score.

1. *Do your own women's listening audit.*
   - Assemble all the data you have in house on women, and screen it for the kind of information that may be serving as company or brand legend. Check to see if it is true or out of date. Be especially careful if you discover research that promises that women always trust you, always think of you as modern, or always turn to you first in the category. Very few brands can sustain that level of respect for a long time without continual renovation and responsiveness.
   - Look out for those presentations that are collecting dust in huge binders on office shelves. They are often dubbed clever names, like "The Future Map of Consumer DNA" or "The Three Horizons of Women." These major tomes may have had their moment in the sun, but I bet few ever resolved the "now what?" issues still on your plate.
   - Look at the way you define and personify your target customer. Typically, customer profiles fall into clichés, such as "she's a go-getter" or "she's confident and happy with who she is." Be on the lookout for collages of photographs that are meant to describe the life she leads. I have seen many photo boards describing impossibly hip women: "She wears clothes from Barney's, drinks cosmopolitans, and loves sushi." Women are not paper-thin sitcom characters. Stereotypes will not lead to excellent creative ideas or media planning. Challenge your marketing team to create a true dimensional profile of your target consumer. Create customer biographies that include her favorite TV shows and movies, her magazine subscriptions, favorite novels, music she loves, ads she likes in other categories, or most often used search engines. This kind of target personification

will help you develop messages that fit in her real media world.

- Make a list of all the questions you have about the women who are your customers. Ask the rest of your team, "What can our customer not live without?" "What frustrates you about our female customers?" "What is the one customer fact you want to be absolutely sure of?" Do not forget to dig into your customer's uniqueness by asking, "What does our customer really look like; how does she live; what makes her laugh; what does she worry about?" That true-to-life picture has to be accurate to begin the listening journey.

2. *Revisit how you collect insights and information from your female customers.* If you are still using focus groups moderated by disinterested moderators and are getting the same rote answers, you may be spending too much money to find out the wrong answers. Focus groups are notorious for homogenizing individual preferences and for catering to the loudest participant while ignoring the quietest one. That is why at Just Ask a Woman we created fresh, personal forums for women, such as our faux TV talk shows or our more intimate Conversations. It is also because we are marketers, not moderators. We listen attentively and loop back to women's opinions throughout the session so that they know we are really interested in what they have to say. The women in our sessions tend to say what they really mean, unlike focus group veterans who realize that they can go through the motions to earn their attendance honorariums. In fact, I overheard a woman—a focus group "professional"— leaving one of our sessions saying, "Wow, I really had to work for my money that time."

    If you are a marketer who depends only on quantitative data, you may be missing the context of why women feel the way they do. You may know what women want from you, but not why or how they want it. Be sure to add the context of ethnographic or in-person discussion to your data. Work with your market research teams to design a listening path that is both intuitive and rational.

3. *Make listening to women a measurable requirement in every department.* If you usually delegate listening to market research or customer service departments, the intelligence can remain isolated there. What if you created a listening task force with listeners from sales, new products, and media? Choose people who are interested in culture and curious about women's nuances and behaviors. Invite them to spread their learning through e-mail bulletins or staff meeting presentations. In addition, do not limit yourself to your own company's expertise. You cannot expect to know everything about women. Call on experts in every field from editorial to anthropology to medicine, money, and fitness. I regularly host Just Ask an Expert Salons for clients and my own business. These sessions draw on the brains of a dozen specially chosen gurus in various fields that are analogous or related to the client's business. It is surprising how much experts from various industries can enhance your business inside precisely because they are outsiders.

4. *Create a vital, rewarded, and active women's consumer advisory board for your brand.* There is no reason to wait until you have a problem to ask women what they want. Choose women from your target audience who are diverse in their lives and opinions, and invite them to come on board as your trusted advisors. They can help you review your plans in development from the very start. Be sure that you decide up front on your distinct charter, goals, and expectations for their involvement as well as a reward system for their help. Assign someone inside or outside your company who will be a consistent contact and absolutely responsible for following up with the consumers. Once women have pledged their interest, the worst outcome would be spotty communications or any dialogue that is not at the

level of your brand voice. At Just Ask a Woman, we help clients create these advisory boards. For instance, we have worked with *Real Simple* magazine to identify women around the country who personify the magazine's attitude. These "wise women" will be featured in articles, or respond to e-mail questions from the magazine's editor.

5. *Make listening to women an every-day discipline.* Not a day goes by that I do not discover something new by observing, eavesdropping, and just paying attention to female customers. What are they wearing? Who are they imitating with their hairstyles, their gestures, or their attitudes? What do they talk about in elevators? How do they interact with store clerks? What TV show reviews do you overhear on the bus? What are teens laughing about as they walk through the mall? I encourage you to listen in restaurants, in waiting lines, and before the movie starts. If you are a woman, listen in fitting rooms and ladies' rooms, and listen to your girlfriends and female relatives and neighbors. There is a wealth of knowledge walking right in front of you. Listening to women is fun, enlightening, and the best way to integrate their real world with your brand. In the end, you will be most successful as a marketer if your best brand listener is you.

Organize for Listening

If your brand was not on the listening track, turning around internal prejudices or closed minds can take some time. Your early steps can even incite some concerns inside your organization. Team members might resist efforts to shift your attention to female consumers, no matter how important they are to your business. However, many of the executives commented throughout this book that one of the ways to be successful with consumers is to be sure that you have women's voices represented on your marketing team. This may require some organizational changes, which sometimes cause fear. I was personally treated to a sort of fearful reaction when I hired and promoted several women at one agency, with one colleague rumoring that I was creating a "Skirt Mafia."

Reaching out to women as customers does not mean alienating men. Nor is putting women at the top of companies and ad agencies a panacea for your problems or a guaranteed route to success. From my experience with dozens of clients, however, a company with no senior women inside will have a tougher time getting it right outside with customers. Marketing requires the best thinking of both genders to be successful.

It is important to address and deal with these gender issues. When a company approaches me to help increase its understanding of the female market, it is a bad sign if their first meeting has only women employees in it. If the men in the company do not feel comfortable with discussing female consumer needs, the project is doomed to fail or to be labeled pink (and therefore not important).

ADVICE ON INCLUDING WOMEN

"Take the politics out of this. Would you do a golf magazine without golfers [on staff]? We keep it honest around here because we have a lot of women in positions of power on the women's magazines. It only takes one brave man to bring a woman up with him to break that glass ceiling. You have to remember there are glass ceilings in every industry, they are just higher or lower depending on the industry you choose. My experience is that it only takes one. Women consumers will reward those companies in leadership positions that will do the heavy lifting, and solve the social problems as well. You can do both. It pays off. It pays off in a big way for us. You can make a lot of money satisfying women."
—Ann Moore, chairman and CEO of Time Inc.

Promoting women is one thing. Encouraging them to be vocal about women is another. If you have a strong representation of women in senior jobs, do you welcome their insights on women? They can be a huge outreach resource right in your midst. In some firms, female employees feel comfortable speaking out as women, and they take advantage of their gender when asked about what female consumers want. In those companies, the culture feels open to their voices, both as professionals and as women.

In other companies, though, "sticking out as a woman" is career suicide. Being one of the guys is the path to success. Work on your internal culture. Be willing to listen to the women inside. If they surface issues with your treatment of female employees, imagine what happens with consumers. At one health insurance company, which was interested in expanding its relationships with female members, the female manager of the project confided that she only got two weeks of paid maternity leave. That was a clear red flag as to the real intent of the company's strategy for women.

Make It Personal

One of the most exciting parts of being a marketer is the ability to integrate your personal intuition and creativity with your professional judgment. I like to start solving business problems with female consumers by asking the women on my team, "What do you think about this in your own life?" I encourage my teams to treat their own customer experiences with the same respect that they give to the research we do.

I heard a story that is an incredible success model for this kind of approach. I was fortunate to meet the team from Oprah's Harpo Productions at a business conference dinner. I asked them how the TV show always manages to come up

with topics that consistently articulate the precise trend or con-
cern that is on women's minds. The women from Harpo answered that, every morning they get together and ask each other
questions like, "What are you hearing? What are you worried
about in your own life? What's funny or scary or inspiring?"

Now, you can imagine that the sustained popularity of the
show attracts the latest, greatest idea from every PR person in the
country. Nonetheless, Oprah and her team depend on their own
judgments and feelings as women to drive the content of the show.
When Oprah found a lump in her breast, she did a show tracking
three women through their chemotherapy and radiation treatment.

Respect Intuition

Women's intuition is rarely heralded, yet it is a vital tool for any
marketer. How often do male marketers turn to their colleagues
and ask, "What's your intuition on this?" My theory is that some
avoid doing it because they do not want the women to feel singled
out from their male colleagues. Women managers may fear that as
well. How often do women in marketing deny their feelings as
women in order to be objective marketers? Marketing is not purely
objective. At best, it is a blend of science and intuition, the very
skill that many women regard as most important in their personal
lives yet often suppress at work. Using your gut is strategic.

The Mission of Marketing with Women

Throughout this book I included interviews with many executives
who have successfully marketed with women. They generously

shared advice on everything from how to communicate to how to listen and how to structure your team for success. The last question I asked each of them was, "What should a marketer always do and never do to create a brand that is chosen by women?" Here is what they said:

Miriam Muley, executive director of marketing and sales at General Motors: "Always ask women. Women are very forthright, and if you put them in an environment where they feel comfortable and not frightened in any way, you can get rich insights from them. Never assume that women are men in dresses. It's not just that we wear different clothes or are genetically structured differently, we really are different. We think differently, we have different needs. Don't market to me as a man and think that I will be your most loyal customer."

Liz Dolan, founder of Satellite Sisters: "There is a tendency among marketers to think there is a whole class of women out there who are different from the women in their lives. If you thought, would I communicate with my sister or my mother this way? Apply the same rules to women as consumers as you do to the women in your lives. If you respect them, you care about their long-term interests, you listen to them and don't shame them or belittle them, that's a really good starting point."

Dan Brestle, president, Estee Lauder: "Never underestimate women. Never underestimate the depth of their curiosity. Challenge the emotional side all the time."

Bonnie Reitz, senior vice president for sales and marketing at Continental Airlines: "Remember that you are in business because there are customers. The customer is always going to get what she wants; she just might not get it from you. Women are your barometers as far as doing it right. Be open to a changing marketplace, and model your products and services accordingly."

Donata Maggipinto, culinary and eating director of Williams-Sonoma: "Marketers tend to overcomplicate things. When women go home, we want things to be as pleasurable as possible. Give me something that will make my life pleasurable, and if you throw in a little fun, that would be good, too. We're holding the families together. It's a huge job we do everyday. Don't talk down to me."

Rob Matteucci, president of the Clairol division at Procter & Gamble: "Never preach at women. It simply doesn't work, and women resent it. Always recognize the role your product plays in their lives and that it is more intricate than for guys. Have conversations with them, give them space to interject their own interpretations, rather than screaming at them and telling them that it is black and white."

Carole Black, president of Lifetime Television: "Always, always value them and realize how incredibly intelligent they are."

Ann Moore, chairman and CEO of Time Inc.: "The most helpful lessons you will ever learn in marketing to women don't come from Harvard Business School. They come from your mother's advice growing up and hold true in the marketplace when you are grown up and marketing to women. Don't forget your homework. Speak up, show up. Look both ways. Listen to your teacher. Nobody cares what happened last week. All the kind of life lessons. What your mother told you was true."

Betta Gallego, vice president of marketing for Dole: "Marketing to women requires honesty. What we have learned the hard way is that you have got to show female consumers role models they can identify with. Women are different, and what you communicate to them can be different for one group than another. But there are some things they have in common. They want to be empowered, they want control over their lives, and to feel confident and feel good. They want some form of escape. And women have a sense of sisterhood that marketers can mine."

Andrea Alstrup, corporate vice president for Johnson & Johnson: "Always try to find a way to understand women and what their needs are. Having an understanding or empathy with women is most important."

Lisa Caputo, president of Citigroup's Women & Co.: "Don't take your existing brochure or pamphlet and put a woman's picture on it. Don't take your existing product and put a pink ribbon on it. Women are smart. They know you are just repackaging to try to appeal to them. Be thoughtful on how you are approaching women and come up with a really unique service or product tailored for them with their input. Be honest about what you're selling. Don't spin it."

Andrea Jung, chairman and CEO of Avon Products: "Combine great listening with good instincts. If you are not listening, if you are not totally aware of what is going on at every front, she'll tell you first. No matter how much you competitive shop, you'll never find it before she does. We are in an environment where the consumer definition of value and quality is changing so fast and furiously. Never be afraid to embrace change."

The Final Lessons Learned

I had a reason for asking the executives the always/never question. It was the same question that I had asked all 3,000 women I have interviewed over the past three years. Here's how I put it to them: "If you were the CEO of this company, what would you always do and never do in order to be an ideal company for women?"

As always, the women were straight with advice and recommendations you can use immediately. There is something about the always/never exercise that compresses women's feelings to the essential truths. The women's answers, more often than not, recommend a code of behavior for marketers. It is especially interesting that their ideas bridge beyond any single category into lessons for all kinds of businesses. Like all the women's words in this book, these are spoken wisely and from the heart. Women simply want marketers to listen to them, to respect them, and to understand them as women.

The Word from Women

In the area of customer service, women want their concerns taken seriously and their needs met directly. "Never pass me off to somebody else. Handle my concerns personally." They want real answers to their questions: "When women have issues, don't just cut us off and Band-Aid our problems." And, they want to be accepted at face value: "Always treat the customer with respect. Never judge her by her appearance."

They recognize their own complexities and wish that marketers would understand: "Women can be emotional, so be compassionate." At the same time, they are as tough as they are vulnerable: "I would just like companies to know that we're confident and we can take care of things. Just give us the tools. Back off and leave us alone, and we'll fix it."

Women wish that marketers would focus on their importance as consumers: "Always keep your eye on the customer, and never keep your eye only on the almighty dollar." In addition, women expect marketers to live up to the same code of conduct they hold themselves to: "If you make a mistake, just own up to it, address it, and try to go the correct way from there."

Women's suggestions always weave their way back to the stress in their lives, since they are adamant about your role as a simplifier: "Always provide easy-to-understand education about your products and procedures in basic terms that anybody can understand." They expect not only that you will know your product, but also that you will be as in love with it as you want them to be: "Be excited about your product, be in love with it, know it well, and make it easy for folks to relate to it."

Their final words of advice relate to communications and relationships: "Never talk down to us," and, "Always respect women as intelligent consumers. We want interaction to give feedback to make better products and services."

As you consider these women's thoughts, I would like to share a behind-the-scenes perspective about the way women answer this question. As soon as I introduce the idea that they assume the role of CEO or head of marketing, you should know that many of them seem to want your job. They smile and sit up confidently and are eager to give their prescriptions for how they wish you would treat them. Their eyes show me that no one ever asked them that question before. The question puts them in charge, and they enjoy the role of being the boss. Ironically, they are the bosses of many of these brands; they just don't know it—yet.

I have also noticed that while they may answer the question as women, their advice is equally good for male customers. Women's ideas rarely favor only women. They conceive human truths. For example, when I interviewed women about business travel, they did not ask for makeup products to be put in the seatback pockets in front of them. They asked for better communication and status updates. They asked that gate agents and counter staff at car rental places listen and solve problems, rather than challenge them, especially when they are running late. That is good customer service, male or female.

I have learned that most women do not think selfishly. They think like the chief marketing officer, who wants to please all customers. The otherness that I described throughout this book applies here and explains why women are a great resource for business problem solving. Do not wait until you have a "woman" problem. Ask them for their help in identifying and resolving any product or service issue, and you will be amazed at their insights.

You should also know that these 3,000 women gave me their ideas generously, but they also quizzed me on whether I was really going to take their opinions forward. As one women said at the close of a session, "Mary Lou, is anyone at that company really going to watch this videotape?" Women are desperate to be heard, but until they see evidence of change, they will be guarded with most people who ask for their honest opinions.

At the risk of adding one more list to those above, I'd like to close with a few of my favorite lessons learned that sum up the path to connecting women to your brand's success. I am grateful to so many people who taught me these lessons. I thank the clients who were willing to take risks. I have learned from the many media leaders who carved out new ways to connect with women. I appreciate the lessons from my agency colleagues who brought a true passion for women to their work. Most of all, I am indebted to the thousands of women who have told me the truths of their lives. This is my way of saying thanks to them, in the hope that more marketers will listen and become successful by understanding their most important customer.

The Last Word from Me

- *Give her a laugh.* She is a professional at taking on others' problems and worries. Give her a little relief. A smile will get you everywhere.

- *Find a way to like her.* Distancing yourself from your female customers makes it difficult to see the world through their eyes. If it is easier to think of your customer as if she were your sister, friend, or mom, do it.

- *Give her space to learn, assess, and decide.* Women decide in their own way at their own pace. Once you have provided the best information about why she should select you, step back and let her choose.

- *Put humanity in the selling process.* Women observe not just what you say and do, but also how. Your competitive advantage can be measured in how much you show that you empathize with her life.

- *Keep the communications simple.* Whether it is written, spoken, e-mailed, or phoned in, speak her language instead of yours.

- *Whenever possible, present a range of diverse women.* Women are keenly aware that there are many lives, lifestyles, and looks among women. They are conscious and caring about the differences. Show her you respect diversity, too.

- *Real beats fantasy. Fantasy beats slapstick. Stupidity loses.* This is a shorthand formula for advertising to women. While each product has its own characteristics and voice, remember that women embrace reality.

- *Consistency, consistency, consistency.* Women's contextual powers of observation and their keen memories will test your total marketing mix. Be sure all elements of reach and communication are as integrated as she is.

- *Ask. Listen. Act.* Women pay attention to the marketers who pay attention to them. Once you ask, be sure to follow up, or you risk burning your newly made bridge to her.

- *And never fall back into stress denial.* It is easy to forget how stressed her life is when yours is too. But every day she tackles another busy agenda, and you have to help her make room on it for your brand. Your stress and her stress are not in a contest.

I believe that the best ideas come from listening, and I would like to extend that listening to you. Please send your always/never ideas to me at marylou@justaskawoman.com. *Just Ask a Woman* is not just a book, a company, or a seminar. It is a way of marketing life. It's easy to take the first step. Just ask.

RESEARCH NOTES

O ver the past three years I have interviewed 3,000 women (and counting) on behalf of clients in nearly every category, from finance to health care, entertainment, beauty, retail, and technology. The interviews were conducted for the purposes of understanding a marketing or communications issue posed by major U.S. and global corporations. The strategic recommendations we provided them are not part of this book; that information was for our clients alone. In this book I searched for the convergent truths that emerged by linking the day in and day out listening to my own years of marketing and communications leadership.

The women were cast differently for every session, thanks to the wide diversity of brands we researched. They ranged from age 18 to 80, with annual household incomes of $25,000 to $250,000. They were married or not, with or without children, and of varying levels of education. These groups of women mirrored the U.S. population in their race and ethnic composition. We listened in 17 U.S. cites in nearly 100 sessions in locations ranging from rural to suburban and major urban areas. I conducted all of the interviews in groups ranging from 8 women to 30 women at a time, for generally two hours in length.

It would be foolish to think that women as a gender have just one way of thinking. The women's beliefs and feelings ranged and shifted depending on the subject and their lives. This book does not mean to paint all women with one brush. I wanted to identify the seven most compelling areas where women were most focused, most convinced, and most passionate so that marketers in every category could find truths to leverage for marketing success.

In addition, this book is the result of in-depth interviews with 19 CEOs and chief marketing officers about what women want and their lessons learned for successfully marketing with women. The following people kindly gave me their time and insights, in addition to Procter & Gamble's chairman and CEO A. G. Lafley, who shared a philosophy that was pivotal to the proposition of this book.

Andrea Alstrup, Corporate Vice President, Johnson & Johnson

Carole Black, President, Lifetime Television

Cathie Black, President, Hearst Magazines

Dan Brestle, President, Estee Lauder

Lisa Caputo, President, Citigroup's Women & Co.

Liz Dolan, Second Sister, Satellite Sisters

Betta Gallego, Vice President, Marketing, Package Foods, Dole

Bob Goehrke, Vice President, Bath and Body Works

Paul Higham, Former Chief Marketing Officer, Wal-Mart

Tom Holliday, President, Retail Advertising and Marketing Association

Christina Johnson, CEO, Saks Fifth Avenue

Andrea Jung, Chairman and CEO, Avon

Dany Levy, Founder, DailyCandy.com

Donata Maggipinto, Culinary Director, Williams-Sonoma

Rob Matteucci, President of Color and Professional Coloring, Clairol, Inc.

Jim McCann, Chairman and CEO, 1800Flowers.com

Ann Moore, Chairman and CEO of Time Inc.

Miriam Muley, Executive Director, General Motors

Bonnie Reitz, Senior Vice President, Sales and Marketing, Continental Airlines

NOTES

Introduction

1. Retrieved from www.ewowfacts.com.
2. Ibid.
3. Ibid.

Chapter Two

1. Retrieved from www.ewowfacts.com.
2. *USA Today*, August 2000.
3. Alexandra Robbins and Abby Wilner, *Quarterlife Crisis: The Unique Challenges of Life in Your Twenties* (New York: Penguin, 2001).
4. Fawn Fitter and Beth Gulas, *Working in the Dark: Keeping Your Job While Dealing with Depression* (Hazelden Information and Educational Services: Washington, D.C., 2002).
5. United States Bureau of the Census, "Labor Force Participation for Mothers with Infants Declines for First Time, Census Bureau Reports." Prepared by the Public Information Office, Washington, DC, October 18, 2001.
6. Linda Villarosa, "Making an Appointment with the Stork," *New York Times*, June 23, 2002, section 15, p. 9.
7. The NICHD Publications On-Line. The National Institute of Child Health and Human Development, "The NICHD Study of Early

Child Care." Prepared by Robin Beth-Pierce in the Public Information and Communications Branch, Washington, DC, 1995.

8. Mary Lou Quinlan, "Advertising to Women Over 40," *MORE*, April 2002, pp. 53–55.

9. Mary Lou Quinlan and Jen Levine, "The Lifetime Report on Women: A Lifetime Television Study." Report presented to Lifetime Television, New York, NY, 2001.

10. Susan Faludi, *Backlash: The Undeclared War against American Women* (New York: Doubleday, 1991).

11. Retrieved from http://www.canoe.ca/LifewiseLiving0203/march14_stressout_c-can.html.

Chapter Three

1. Retrieved from www.bcentral.com.

Chapter Four

1. Retrieved May 9, 2002, from www.money.cnn.com.

2. Retrieved July 1, 2002, from http://shoppingcenterworld.com.

3. Helen Fisher, *The First Sex: The Natural Talents of Women and How They Are Changing the World* (Random House: New York, 1999).

4. Turhan Canli, John E. Desmond, Zuo Zhao, and John D. E. Gabrieli, "Sex Differences in the Neural Basis of Emotional Memories," *Proceedings of the National Academy of Sciences*, vol. 99, no. 16 (July 2002), 10789–10794.

5. Retrieved from www.womanmotorist.com.

6. Fara Warner, "Nike's Women's Movement," *Fast Company*, vol. 61 (August 2002), 70.

7. Ibid.

8. Ron Lieber, "I Take Thee . . . Back to the Store," *Wall Street Journal*, May 30, 2002, p. D1.

Chapter Five

1. Didi Gluck, "Better at 40, than 20," *Marie Claire*, July 2002, p. 51.

2. Retrieved from www.womanmotorist.com.

3. Alex Kuczynski, "Teenage Magazines Mostly Reject Breast Enlargement Ads," *New York Times*, cection C, p. 1.

4. Retrieved May 24, 2001, from www.cottoninc.com.

5. Retrieved January 22, 2001, from www.aarp.org.

Chapter Six

1. Retrieved June 15, 2001, from www.nua.com.

2. AOL/Roper ASW Cyberstudy 2001. Retrieved from www.wit.org.

3. Retrieved April 18, 2002, from www.nua.com.

4. Retrieved from www.herhifi.com.

5. Michael Sehau, et al. *All About Women Consumers*, 2000 edition. (New York: EPM Communications, Inc., 2000, p. 231).

6. Michael Sehau, ed., *All About Women Consumers* (New York: EPM Communications, Inc., 2000).

7. *USA Today* article, 1998. Retrieved from ewowfacts.com.

8. Joan Meyers-Levy, "How Men and Women Differ Their Responses to Marketing Messages," *Capital Ideas*, vol.1, no. 3 (1998), p. 4.

9. Retreived from www.ewowfacts.com.

10. Biff Burns for Burst! Media. Burst! Media Proprietary Research, May 2002.

11. Ron Lieber, "Operator, I Demand an Automated Menu," *Wall Street Journal*, July 30, 2002, p. D1.

Chapter Seven

1. Retrieved from www.ewowfacts.com.

2. Ibid.

3. Ibid.

4. Mary Lou Quinlan and Jen Levine, "The Lifetime Report on Women: A Lifetime Television Study." Report presented to Lifetime Television, New York, NY, 2001.

5. Retrieved from www.cnn.com.

6. Michael Sehau, *All About Women Consumers* (New York: EPM Communications, Inc., 2000, p. 64).

7. Retrieved from www.ewowfacts.com.

8. Retrieved from www.digitrends.net.

9. Retrieved from www.nfwbo.org.

10. Retrieved from www.nfwbo.org.

11. Retrieved from www.saks.com.

12. Retrieved from www.avon.com.

Chapter Eight

1. Press release, "Survey Shows Single, Married Women Debunking Home Improvement's Male Image." Retrieved from www.lowes.com.

2. Eisenberg, "Trends in Alternative Medicine Use in the United States, 1990–1997," *Journal of American Medical Association*, vol. 280 (1998), 1569–1575.

3. "Public Attitudes Towards Massage Study" [Caravan Study], Opinion Research Corporation International (July 2001).

INDEX